HYMNS
ON
PARADISE

HYMNS ON PARADISE

ST EPHREM

Introduction and translation
by
SEBASTIAN BROCK

ST VLADIMIR'S SEMINARY PRESS
CRESTWOOD, NEW YORK 10707
1998

Library of Congress Cataloging-in-Publication Data

Ephraem, Syrus, Saint, 303-373.
    [Hymni de paradiso. English]
    Hymns on paradise / St. Ephrem the Syrian;
[commentary] by Sebastian Brock; with translation from Syriac by
Sebastian Brock
    p.   cm.
    Translation of: Hymni de paradiso and Section 2 of
Commnetarium in Genesium.
    Includes bibliographical references.
    ISBN 0-88141-076-4
    1. Paradise—Early works to 1800.   2. Hymns,
Syriac—Translations into English—Early works to 1800
3. Bible. O.T. Genesis II-III-Commentaries   I. Brock, Sebastian
P. II. Ephraem, Syrus, Saint, 303-373. Commentarium in
Genesim. Section 2. English. 1989. III. Title.
BR65.E633H9613   1990
264'.01402—dc20

                  89-37281
                  CIP
                  r89

Translation © 1990

ST VLADIMIR'S SEMINARY PRESS
575 Scarsdale Rd., Crestwood, NY 10707
1-800-204-2665

ISBN 0-88141-076-4

PRINTED IN THE UNITED STATES OF AMERICA

Table of Contents

1.
INTRODUCTION

To many people St Ephrem the Syrian will be known best for the beautiful prayer, attributed to him, used during the Lenten Fast[1]:

O Lord and Master of my life, give me not a spirit of sloth, vain curiosity, lust for power, and idle talk, but give to me Thy servant a spirit of soberness, humility, patience, and love. O Lord and King, grant me to see my own faults and not to condemn my brother: for blessed art Thou to the ages of ages. Amen. O God, cleanse me a sinner.

But Ephrem also happens to be a religious poet of quite outstanding stature, one who deserves to rank alongside the greatest of theologian poets in the Christian tradition. That he has only rarely been recognized as such is due largely to the inaccessibility of his works, written in Syriac (a dialect of Aramaic) and for the most part poorly served by translations into modern languages. Indeed it is only within the last thirty or so years that reliable editions of the original texts of his works have appeared, thanks to the labors of Dom Edmund Beck, O.S.B.

---

[1]*The Lenten Triodion* (translated by Mother Mary and Archimandrite Kallistos Ware; London and Boston, 1978), pp. 69-70.

It is with the aim of making up, in a small way, for this
deficiency as far as English is concerned, that the present
translation is offered. The cycle of fifteen hymns on Paradise
has been chosen since it offers a fine example of the way
in which St Ephrem is able to weave a profound theological synthesis organized around a particular Biblical
narrative, in this case Genesis chapters 2 and 3. By penetrating beyond the letter of the text he succeeds in drawing
out its inner meaning and in relating this to the Christian
message as a whole; all this he achieves through the medium
of poetry, not the vehicle we usually associate with theological writing today, but which nonetheless is capable of
conveying theological insights in a manner that is at once
dynamic and compelling. Who then was this remarkable
man?

The Life of St Ephrem

On the surface it might appear that this fourth-century
saint's life was extremely well documented, for there exist
not only biographies in both Greek and Syriac, but also
a variety of texts which claim to be autobiographical, most
notable among them being a Testament. The majority of
these texts, however, do not stand up well under any
critical examination, and the Syriac biography in particular
can be shown to be a comparatively late work, written in
the sixth century, at least 150 years after St Ephrem's
death, and full of unhistorical material, such as visits to
St Basil in Cappadocia and to St Bishoi in Egypt.

In order, then, to gain some reasonably reliable picture
of St Ephrem, it will be wisest to treat the biographical
references chronologically in order of their appearance.

First and foremost come the very rare allusions in St
Ephrem's genuine works. Two passages imply that his

parents were Christian: in the last stanza of Hymn XXVI
Against the Heresies he writes:

> These two things belong to our Lord:
> the time when I was to enter into the created world
> and when it will be beneficial for me to leave it.
> I was born in the path of truth,
> even though my childhood was unaware;
> but once I grew aware I acquired it in the furnace.[2]
> The crooked paths that I came across
> did my faith spurn,
> for they led to the position on the left [Matthew 25:33].
> Because I have acknowledged You, Lord, do You
>   acknowledge me;
> have compassion on this sinner who has believed in You,
> for even if he sins, he still knocks at Your door,
> even if he is sluggish, he still travels on Your road.

A similar passage occurs in the Hymns on Virginity,
XXXVII.10:

> Your truth was with me in my youth,
> Your faithfulness is with my old age.

From a cycle of hymns on the town of Nisibis (on the
easternmost frontier of the Roman Empire, modern Nusey-
bin in southeast Turkey) we learn that St Ephrem served
as a deacon and catechetical teacher under a series of remarkable bishops. The first of these was St Jacob of Nisibis,
one of the "318" Fathers who attended the Council of

---

[2]This is probably an allusion to his baptism: the font is frequently
referred to as a furnace in Syriac baptismal tradition (the Syrian
Orthodox baptismal service speaks of "the renewal of Adam, God's
image, in the furnace of baptism"); see S. P. Brock, *The Holy Spirit
in the Syrian Baptismal Tradition* (*Syrian Churches Series* 9, 1979),
pp. 13, 135.

Nicaea in 325. It was on Jacob's return home that, according to a late sixth-century writer,[3] he appointed Ephrem to a teaching position. Jacob, who died in 338 or shortly after, was followed by Babu (c. 338-50), Vologeses (c. 350-361) and Abraham (c. 361-?). During these years Nisibis was besieged on three separate occasions (338, 346 and 350) by the Persian army. The last of these sieges was particularly dramatic, for the Persian king Shapur II dammed the local river in order to flood the surroundings of the town; the first of Ephrem's Nisibene hymns describes this event, and compares the town to Noah's Ark floating on the waters of the Flood: Nisibis herself speaks in stanza 3,

> All kinds of storms trouble me
>   and I count the Ark fortunate:
> only waves surrounded it,
>   but ramps and arrows as well as waves surround me.
> The Ark acted as a store for treasure for You,
>   but I have become a deposit of sins.
> The Ark subdued the waves through Your love,
>   whereas I have been blinded amidst the arrows
>   through Your anger.
> The Flood bore the Ark,
>   while me the river threatens.
> O Helmsman of the Ark,
>   be my pilot on dry land;
> You rested the Ark on the haven of a mountain,
>   give rest to me too in the haven of my walls.

The city survived all three sieges and once hostilities between the two empires had subsided Bishop Vologeses was able to undertake some notable building enterprises. A

---

[3]Barhadbeshabba of Ḥalwan, *The Origin of the Schools*, in *Patrologia Orientalis* 4, p. 63. For the early bishops of Nisibis see J-M. Fiey, *Nisibe* (CSCO 388 = Subsidia 54, 1977), pp. 21-36.

baptistery of remarkably fine workmanship[4] survives to this day incorporated into the Church of St Jacob of Nisibis (whose crypt still houses the tomb of St Jacob). The building's original function and the date are recorded in Greek in an inscription which reads as follows:

> This baptistery was erected and completed in the year 671 [= A.D. 359/60] in the time of Bishop Volageses through the zeal of the priest Akepsimas. May this inscription be a memorial to them.

We thus have a direct link with a building in which St Ephrem will have functioned as deacon.

In 363 the emperor Julian was killed in the course of a Roman incursion into Persian territory, and as part of the ensuing peace treaty Nisibis was handed over to the Persians. The historian Ammianus Marcellinus informs us that one of the conditions laid down was that the Christian population of Nisibis should leave. Among the numerous refugees was St Ephrem, perhaps now in his late fifties. In due course he made his new home in Edessa (modern Urfa), some 100 miles further west, and it was there that he spent the last decade of his life. Many of Ephrem's hymns and prose works clearly belong to his time at Edessa, for they reflect the more hellenized culture of that town and the intellectual ferment brought about by speculative theological thinking among the followers of Marcion, Bardaisan of Edessa, Mani, Arius and others; much of Ephrem's energy was expended on combating these perversions of the faith.

While the year of St Ephrem's birth is not known, that of his death is certain, 373. The precise date, however, is variously given, but perhaps most likely to be correct is

---

[4]See G. Bell (ed. M. M. Mango), *The Churches and Monasteries of the Tur 'Abdin* (London, 1982), pp. 142-5, plates 70-83.

June 9th, provided by the sixth-century Chronicle of Edessa (the 15th, 18th and 19th of June are the dates given in other sources).

The earliest external witness[5] to St Ephrem and his literary activity is provided by St Jerome in his book on famous men, written in 392, nineteen years after St Ephrem's death; here he tells us that "Ephrem, a deacon of the Church of Edessa, wrote a great deal in the Syriac language. He attained such distinction that his writings are read in some churches after the Scriptural lections. I have read a work of his on the Holy Spirit, which someone had translated from Syriac into Greek, and even in translation I could recognize the acumen of a lofty intellect."

Next in date is Palladius' *Lausiac History* (419/20), in which chapter 40 is devoted to St Ephrem. Here it is interesting to find the earliest portrayal of Ephrem as a monk (Palladius speaks of "his cell"), but as we shall see, this is an anachronistic feature, since St Ephrem probably only came into contact with Egyptian-style monasticism right at the end of his life. Palladius' descriptions of his efforts at famine relief, however, are very probably reliable. The following translation is made from the early Syriac version of the *Lausiac History;* the translator has added at both the beginning and the end material which is absent from the Greek (paragraphs 1 and 3 below):[6]

---

[5]It has sometimes been supposed that "the Syrian" mentioned by St Basil in his second homily on the Hexaemeron is to be identified with St Ephrem, but this is most unlikely; it was, however, probably on the basis of such an identification that Sozomen (in a passage quoted below) stated that St Basil greatly admired St Ephrem. Later tradition held that the two saints actually met (see note 12).

[6]Translated from R. Draguet's edition in CSCO 398 = Scriptores Syri 173, pp. 286-9 (for parallels to the translator's additions see Draguet's French translation in CSCO 399 = Scr. Syri 174, p. 190). On St Ephrem and monasticism, see below.

One of the Holy Fathers saw in a dream a band of holy angels come down from heaven at God's behest. One of them was holding in his hand a scroll written both on the inside and on the outside. They were asking each other, "To whom should this be entrusted?" Some of them said to one particular person, while others to another; yet others, however, said "These people are indeed saints and upright, but they are not capable of being entrusted with it." Having mentioned the names of many other saints, they finally said, "No one can be entrusted with this apart from Ephrem." Thereupon they gave it to him. When the father arose in the morning he heard people saying, "Ephrem teaches as if a fountain was flowing from his mouth." Then the elder who had seen the dream recognized that what issued from his lips was from the Holy Spirit.

This Ephrem is one of the saints who is worthy of mention. He journeyed excellently and uprightly along the spiritual path, never turning to either side from the straight path. He was held worthy of natural knowledge, and subsequently of the divine, and of perfect beatitude.[7] Having continually lived a chaste life in quietude for a specific number of years, edifying in a variety of different ways all those who came to visit him, he eventually felt compelled to leave his cell for the following reason: a dire famine weighed down on the town of Edessa, and in his compassion for the condition of the people who were wasting away and perishing, observing that those who were hoarding grain in their storehouses had no sense of pity, he addressed them as follows: "How long will you fail to pay attention to God's compassion, allowing

---

[7]Palladius here quotes from Evagrius' prologue to his *Praktikos* (ed. Guillaumont, *Sources chrétiennes* 171, p. 492).

your wealth to be corrupted, to the condemnation and damnation of your own souls?" They decided among themselves to say to him, "We have no one we can trust with providing for those who are dying of starvation; for everyone is dishonest, and will act in an underhand way." Ephrem replied, "What opinion do you have of me?" for he had a great reputation with everyone, in a quite genuine and unfeigned way. They answered, "We know you are a man of God." "In that case," he said, "entrust me with the business; I will devote myself to becoming a hostel manager." Having received some money he began to shut off suitable areas in the streets, and saw to the provision of three hundred beds; some of these were to be used for burying those who had died; while other were for those who still had some hope of life to lie upon. Furthermore, he also had all those suffering from starvation in the villages brought in and given beds. He spent every day in constant attendance on them, seeing to their every need with great caring, making use of the means available to him. This he did joyfully, with the help of those whom he had asked to assist in the matter.[8] When that year of famine had passed, and the following year was one of plenty, everyone returned home, there being nothing left to do. Ephrem then went back to his cell and ended his life a month later, God having provided this means of crowning the end of his life. He left many books and various compositions worthy of careful attention.

It is said of him that when he was a boy he saw a dream—or a vision—in which a vine shoot sprung up from his tongue; it grew and everywhere under the

---

[8]The Greek text is rather shorter at this point and contains no mention of the relief work being extended to the villages: perhaps this information was based on local memories of the event.

heavens was filled by it; it bore bunches of grapes in proliferation, and all the birds of the sky came and ate of its fruits; the more they ate, the more the bunches multiplied and grew.

There is no reason to doubt the historicity of the narrative about St Ephrem's role in the famine, and it is significant that the chronological details at the end of this paragraph fit well with the date given in the Chronicle of Edessa for his death, June 9th; the year of famine will have run from the failure of the wheat harvest (no doubt due to drought) in early summer 372 to the first grain crop (barley) of 373, harvested in early May.

Some twenty or more years after Palladius wrote his *Lausiac History* the church historian Sozomen devoted an interesting chapter to St Ephrem, which is worth quoting almost in full, despite its length.[9]

Ephrem the Syrian was entitled to the highest honors, and was the greatest ornament of the catholic Church. He was a native of Nisibis, or his family was of the neighboring territory. He devoted his life to monastic philosophy; and although he received no instruction, he became, contrary to all expectation, so proficient in the learning and language of the Syrians, that he comprehended with ease the most abstruse theorems of philosophy. His style of writing was so filled with splendid oratory and with richness and temperateness of thought that he surpassed the most approved writers of Greece. If the works of these writers were to be translated into Syriac, or any other

---

[9]Ecclesiastical History III.16. I use C. D. Hartranft's translation in *A Select Library of Nicene and Post-Nicene Fathers,* series II, vol. 2 (Oxford and New York, 1891), with a few small modifications. In VI.34 Sozomen again mentions St Ephrem, among notable monastic figures from the Edessa area.

language, and divested, as it were, of the beauties of
the Greek language, they would retain little of their
original elegance and value. The productions of
Ephrem have not this disadvantage: they were translated into Greek during his life, and translations are
even now being made, and yet they preserve much
of their original force, so that his works are not less
admired when read in Greek than when read in
Syriac. Basil, who was subsequently bishop of the
metropolis of Cappadocia, was a great admirer of
Ephrem, and was astonished at his erudition. The
opinion of Basil, who is universally confessed to have
been the most eloquent man of his age, is a stronger
testimony, I think, to the merit of Ephrem, than anything that could be indited to his praise. It is said
that he wrote three hundred thousand verses, and
that he had many disciples who were zealously attached to his doctrines. The most celebrated of his
disciples were Abbas, Zenobius, Abraham, Maras,
and Simeon, in whom the Syrians and whoever among
them pursued accurate learning make a great boast.
Paulonas and Aranad are praised for their finished
speech, although they are reported to have deviated
from sound doctrine.

I am not ignorant that there were some very learned
men who formerly flourished in Osrhoene, as, for
instance, Bardaisan, who devised a heresy designated
by his name, and Harmonius, his son. It is related
that this latter was deeply versed in Greek erudition,
and was the first to subdue his native tongue to
metres and musical laws; these verses he delivered to
the choirs, and even now the Syrians frequently sing,
not the precise copies by Harmonius, but the same
melodies. For as Harmonius was not altogether free
from the errors of his father, and entertained various
opinions concerning the soul, the generation and the

destruction of the body, and the regeneration which are taught by the Greek philosophers, he introduced some of these ideas into the lyrical songs which he composed. When Ephrem perceived that the Syrians were charmed with the elegance of the diction and the rhythm of the melody, he became apprehensive, lest they should imbibe the same opinions; and therefore, although he was ignorant of Greek learning, he applied himself to the understanding of the metres of Harmonius, and composed similar poems in accordance with the doctrines of the Church, and wrote also sacred hymns and the praises of passionless men. From that period the Syrians sang the odes of Ephrem according to the law of the ode established by Harmonius. The execution of this work is alone sufficient to attest the natural endowments of Ephrem.

He was as celebrated for the good actions he performed as for the rigid course of discipline he pursued. He was particularly fond of tranquility. He was so serious and so careful to avoid giving occasion to calumny, that he refrained from the very sight of women. It is related that a female of careless life, who was either desirous of tempting him, or who had been bribed for the purpose, contrived on one occasion to meet him face to face, and fixed her eyes intently on him; he rebuked her, and commanded her to look down upon the ground. "Why should I obey your injunction," replied the woman, "for I was born not of the earth, but of you? It would be more just if you were to look down upon the earth from which you sprang, while I look upon you, as I was born of you." Ephrem, astonished at the woman, recorded the whole matter in a book, which most Syrians regard as one of the best of his productions.[10]

---

[10]No extant work by Ephrem mentions such an episode.

It is also said of him that, although he was naturally prone to passion, he never exhibited angry feeling toward anyone from the period of his embracing a monastic life. It once happened that after he had, according to custom, been fasting several days, his attendant, in presenting some food to him, let fall the dish on which it was placed. Ephrem, seeing that he was overwhelmed with shame and fear, said to him, "Take courage; we will go to the food as the food does not come to us"; and he immediately seated himself beside the fragments of the dish, and ate his supper.

What I am about to relate will suffice to show that he was totally exempt from the love of vainglory. He was appointed bishop of some town, and attempts were made to convey him away for the purpose of ordaining him. As soon as he became aware of what was intended, he ran to the marketplace, and showed himself as a madman by stepping in a disorderly way, dragging his clothes along, and eating in public. Those who had come to carry him away to be their bishop, on seeing him in this state, believed that he was out of his mind, and departed; and he, meeting with an opportunity for effecting his escape, remained in concealment until another had been ordained in his place.

What I have now said concerning Ephrem must suffice, although his own countrymen relate many other anecdotes of him. Yet his conduct on one occasion, shortly before his death, appears to me so worthy of remembrance that I shall record it here.

At this point Sozomen gives an account of Ephrem's charitable work during the famine; since Sozomen has drawn closely on Palladius' narrative for this, the section is omitted here. Sozomen then continues:

He attained no higher clerical order than that of deacon, although he became no less famous for his virtue than those who are ordained to the priesthood and are admired for the conversation of a good life and for learning. I have now given some account of the virtue of Ephrem.

Much in Sozomen's chapter is positively misleading: he develops the false hint already given by Palladius that Ephrem was a monk (the ascetic ideals by which Ephrem almost certainly did live are discussed below); he gives an account of the origins of Syriac hymnography which is likely to be both tendentious and incorrect[11]; and his portrait of Ephrem as shunning the face of women hardly conforms with the great tenderness for, and understanding of, women that St Ephrem's genuine writings exhibit, or with the fact that he wrote many of his hymns specifically for women's choirs (this is evident on internal grounds as well as from the testimony of Jacob of Serugh, quoted below). All this makes it very unlikely that any reliance can be placed on the story of how he avoided being consecrated a bishop; this very probably arose out of an attempt to explain why he never advanced beyond the rank of deacon.

Theodoret's *Ecclesiastical History,* written ca. 449/50, likewise contains a chapter on Ephrem (IV.29). Whereas in Sozomen the section on Ephrem follows one on Didymus the Blind, Theodoret couples the two writers; what he has to say about Ephrem is quite short, and confined to the fame of his verse compositions. Theodoret would appear to be drawing almost entirely on Sozomen (or, possibly, a common source), though he does add that Ephrem's hymns were still used in his day at festivals in honor of the martyrs. Earlier in the *Ecclesiastical History* (II.30),

---

[11]See below, on "Poetic Form."

when narrating the life of St Jacob of Nisibis, Theodoret states that it was Ephrem who urged Jacob to mount the city walls during the siege of 338 and rebuke the Persian King Shapur II for his blasphemy. In the *Historia Philothea,* however, where the same episode is recounted, no mention is made of Ephrem's role.

From the end of the fifth century we have another short notice in Latin, given by Gennadius in his supplement to Jerome's book on famous men. Chapter 3, which is really about Ephrem's disciple Paulonas, reads as follows:

> The priest Paulonas, a disciple of the blessed Ephrem the deacon, was a man of keen intellect and learned in the divine Scriptures. While his master was alive he was famous among the Doctors of the Church, especially as an orator, but after Ephrem's death, out of love for high position and fame, he separated himself from the Church and wrote a great deal against the faith. It is said that on his death-bed the blessed Ephrem addressed him with this warning: "Paulonas, see that you do not give way to your own imaginings; when you think you have attained to an understanding of God, then believe that you have not understood at all." For Ephrem sensed from his studies and writings that he would track out novel ideas and stretch his intellectual powers to the limit, for which reason Ephrem often called him "the new Bardaisan."

Later, in chapter 67, Gennadius makes passing mention of "Ephrem the deacon's poem on the destruction of Nicomedia" (by earthquake on the 24th of August 358). This is a work which survives complete only in an Armenian translation.

With the Syriac life we are already well into the sixth century, for, thanks to a topographical detail concerning the course of the river Daisan around (and not through) Edessa, we can be sure that this life dates from at least the third decade of the sixth century, for it presupposes the diversion of the river Daisan sponsored by the emperor Justinian in the aftermath of a disastrous flood in April 525.

Not surprisingly the author of this life (which comes down to us in three slightly different forms) draws heavily on the information provided by earlier writers. What he has to add that is new is unfortunately of no historical value. Thus, for example, Ephrem is made out to be the child of a pagan priest—something which can hardly be squared with Ephrem's own declaration that he was brought up "in the way of truth." Equally unhistorical are his travels to Egypt to visit St Bishoi (Pisoes), and to Cappadocia to visit St Basil. This latter, well-known, episode, where St Ephrem is miraculously endowed with the ability to speak Greek, is probably an elaboration of the identification, first encountered in Sozomen, of the anonymous "Syrian," mentioned by St Basil, with St Ephrem.[12] The account in the Syriac life ends with a serious anachronism, since it describes St Basil as dying before St Ephrem: in fact he died in 379, six years after Ephrem's death.

Despite the unhistorical character of the episode of St Ephrem's meeting with St Basil, it does reflect some truth on quite a different plane, in that the theological interests and message of the two Fathers, although expressed in outwardly very different ways, are remarkably similar. (The similarity in fact extends to others of the Cappadocian Fathers, notably St Gregory of Nyssa).

---

[12]On the episode see O. Rousseau, "La rencontre de S. Ephrem et de S. Basile," *L'Orient Syrien* 2 (1957), pp. 261-84, and 3 (1958), pp. 73-90. Although unhistorical, the meeting of these two great saints does correctly express, at a different level, the underlying harmony between their two separate theological approaches.

The Greek lives, three of which are printed in volume 1 of the great eighteenth-century edition of St Ephrem's works, contain little or nothing that is of historical value, and so are passed over here. The same applies to the various Syriac texts which purport to be autobiographical; earliest among these, but probably not even with a genuine core, is the Testament.

One further source should be mentioned here, the verse panegyric on St Ephrem by the chorepiskopos Jacob of Serugh, next after Ephrem perhaps the greatest of Syriac poets (although writing in a very different style). Since Jacob died in 521, his poem will date from before the composition of the Syriac prose life. As might be expected, his poem contains little historical material. Jacob sees Ephrem above all as someone who combined both words and actions[13]:

> A true worker who labored diligently from start to finish,
> manifesting in himself both words and actions in a
>   practical way,
> he was an architect who built upon the foundation of
>   truth,
> finishing off his edifices with gold and precious stones.
> He was the teacher of truth who both acted and taught,
>   as it is written;
> for his disciples he depicted a model for them to imitate.
> . . . He did not just teach through the toil of speech,
> but he manifested in his own person the activity of
>   perfect sainthood.

But more interesting is what Jacob has to say about Ephrem as a poet who wrote specifically for women. Two passages in particular are worth quoting[14]:

---

[13]Edited by P. Bedjan, *Acta Martyrum et Sanctorum,* (Paris and Leipzig, 1892), pp. 667, 677.

[14]Pp. 668, 672.

The wise Moses made the virgins
not to hold back from the praise that was requisite,
so too Ephrem, who proved a second Moses for women
  folk,
taught them to sing praise with the sweetest of songs.

And, in more detail,

The blessed Ephrem saw that the women were silent
  from praise
and in his wisdom he decided it was right that they
  should sing out;
so just as Moses gave timbrels to the young girls,
thus did this discerning man compose hymns for virgins.
As he stood among the sisters it was his delight
to stir these chaste women into songs of praise;
he was like an eagle perched among the doves
as he taught them to sing new songs of praise with
  pure utterance.
Flocks of meek partridge surrounded him,
learning how to sing a sweet song in purity of voice;
he taught the swallows to warble
and the Church resounded with the lovely sound of
  chaste women's voices.
This is what Ephrem said to the pure women
as he instructed them how to sing praise:
"O daughters of the nations, approach and learn a new
  form of praise
to Him who has delivered you from the error of your
  ancestors;
you have been rescued from the worship of dead idols,
so give praise to Him by whose death you were freed.
You put on the robe of praise from the Font, as did
  your brothers,
and from the single Chalice did you receive new life
  along with them.

You and they have experienced a single salvation, so
  why then
have you not learned to sing praise with a loud voice?
Your voice has been silent because your mother Eve
  closed it,
but now, through your sister Mary, it has been opened
  again to give praise.
Whereas the aged Eve devised a stone of silence for
  your tongue,
her young daughter has undone the bonds so that you
  can shout out;
the married Eve placed a muzzle of silence on your
  mouths,
but the Virgin has opened the closed door with your
  hosannas.
Up till now you women folk have been cast down
  because of Eve,
but henceforth through Mary you are restored again to
  sing glory.
As a result of the wicked act of your mother Eve were
  you kept veiled,
but now through the Child of your sister Mary you
  have been given freedom,
so uncover your faces to sing praise, without feeling
  ashamed,
to Him who, by being born, caused you to acquire
  freedom of speech.

Jacob ends his poem[15] by comparing St Ephrem to

a sheepdog guarding the sheep of God's household,
building for them a sheepfold out of his poems and
  hymns,
so that, within their safety, he might guard the sheep
  from storms;

---

[15]P. 679.

at the same time he scatters, by means of his compelling
   songs,
the heresies that rove around like wild animals outside.

It is attractive to suppose that when Jacob wrote these
words he had in mind the various passages in St Ephrem's
poems where the poet speaks of himself as one of the dogs
waiting under the table to catch any crumbs that might
fall (Matthew 15:27).

St Ephrem and Monasticism

In one of the few early depictions of St Ephrem, in an
eleventh-century collection of Syriac homilies, he and
Jacob of Serugh are depicted in monastic habit.[16] As far
as St Ephrem is concerned, such a depiction is anachronistic, for he was certainly never a monk in what later became the standard sense of the word. As we have already
seen, Palladius appears to have been the first person to
imply that Ephrem was a monk, and subsequent writers,
notably Sozomen and the later lives, simply develop this
idea. In fact, however, Ephrem probably only came across
tributaries of Egyptian monasticism right at the end of his
life during his last years at Edessa;[17] he was certainly never
a member of any such community. Rather, Ephrem will

---

[16]Illustrated in J. Leroy, *Les manuscrits syriaques à peintures*,
II (Paris, 1964), plate 61.

[17]So E. Beck, "Ascétisme et monachisme chez saint Ephrem,"
L'Orient Syrien 3 (1958), pp. 273-98. A different view is taken by
A. Vööbus, who accepts as genuine certain works which Beck
(rightly) rejects as spurious: see, for example, his *History of
Asceticism in the Syrian Orient*, II (CSCO 197 = Subsidia 17)
pp. 70-110. Cf also S. P. Brock, *The Luminous Eye: The Spiritual
World Vision of St Ephrem* (Rome, 1985) ch. 8.

have belonged to the native Syrian ascetic tradition which developed its own brand of what one might call "proto-monasticism." Central to this ascetic tradition was the ideal lying behind the term *ihidaya,* a word covering a whole variety of different meanings, "single," "celibate," "single-minded," "simple" (in the sense of straightforward), and most importantly "a follower or imitator of Christ the *Ihidaya* or "Only-Begotten." Only after Egyptian monasticism had reached north Syria and Mesopotamia in the last decades of the fourth century did the term *ihidaya* come to take on the sense of *monachos,* or "monk," and sometimes also "solitary."

It would appear that by St Ephrem's time the term *ihidaya* normally included two categories of people, the *bthule,* "virgins," both men and women (in other words, celibates), and the *qaddishe,* or married people who had renounced marital intercourse. The latter term, literally meaning "holy" or "sanctified," had taken its origin from Exodus 19, verses 10 and 15. Together these groups constituted *qyama,* conventionally translated "covenant," and they were known as the "members (literally "children") of the covenant."[18] Evidently they had undertaken certain ascetic vows at their baptism (which would still have usually been in adulthood), and they lived in small groups or communes serving the local church in a variety of different ways. It would seem that, unlike Egyptian monasticism, this Syrian proto-monasticism was essentially an urban or village phenomenon.

This ascetic ideal of virginity did not stem from dualist denigration of the "flesh," implying that it was inherently evil, but rather was based on three powerful conceptual models.

---

[18]Other meanings such as "pact," "promise," "stance," and "position" are also possible. A good survey is provided by G. Nedungatt, "The Convenanters of the early Syriac-speaking Church," *Orientalia Christiana Periodica* 39 (1973), pp. 191-215, 419-44.

First and foremost comes the idea of Christ as the Bridegroom, based on several New Testament parables, notably that of the Wise and Foolish Virgins (Matthew 25). From an early date the Church came to be described as the Bride of Christ, and in the liturgical texts of the Syriac Churches her betrothal to Christ is seen as taking place at Christ's baptism. An early hymn for Epiphany opens[19]:

My imagination wafted me to the Jordan
    where I beheld a wonder
when the glorious Bridegroom was revealed
    to make a marriage feast for the Bride and to
    sanctify her.

The Semitic mentality of the biblical writers and of the Syriac poets, such as St Ephrem, finds it very easy to move from the collective to the individual, and from the individual to the collective. Thus Adam is regularly seen both as an individual and as humanity as a whole; this may even be found within the limits of a single short passage, as is the case in one of St Ephrem's Hymns on the Fast (II.4):

Blessed is He who put on Adam
and by means of the Wood of the Cross
made him leap back into Paradise.

By adopting this mode of thinking, it is easy to see how every individual member of the Church, as well as the Church as a collective, could be regarded as the Bride of Christ. In the New Testament parables the marriage feast

---

[19]Edited by E. Beck in CSCO 186 = Scriptores Syri 82, p. 217. The hymn is known to both East and West Syrian liturgical tradition and takes the form of a dialogue between John the Baptist and Christ; on it see "Dialogue hymns of the Syriac Churches," *Sobornost/Eastern Churches Review* 5 (1983), pp. 35-45, and *Le Muséon* 97 (1984), pp. 44-5.

and the bridal chamber (*gnona*)[20] belong to the eschaton
and the second coming; in the life of the Church, however,
this second coming can also be understood as being anticipated (as it were) in Christ's presence in the Eucharist, and
it is in this context that St Ephrem juxtaposes the idea of
the individual soul and the collective Church as brides of
Christ:[21]

> The soul is Your bride, the body Your bridal chamber,
> Your guests are the senses and the thoughts.
> And if a single body is a wedding feast for You,
> how great is Your banquet for the whole Church!

Here, with deliberate paradox, the poet speaks of Christ
the Bridegroom entering the bridal chamber of the body,
where the bride, the soul, is already residing—a remarkable
illustration of the very positive attitude of St Ephrem toward the body. Here of course the imagery has been in-
teriorized, but it is clear that behind the ideal of virginity
lay a more literalist interpretation which regarded any
marital union as an adulterous breaking of the promise of
betrothal to Christ, seen originally as having been made
at baptism. In St Ephrem's elder contemporary, Aphrahat
"the Persian Sage," we encounter a remarkable interpretation of Genesis 2:24 which provides a rationale for such a
view[22]: commenting on the words "Therefore a man leaves

---

[20]The New Testament basis for the term is provided by Matthew
25:10 (although the extant Syriac translations use a different word,
early writers regularly quote the verse using the term *gnōnā*, e.g.
Aphrahat, *Demonstration* VI.1). Cf. also *The Luminous Eye*,
chs. 3, 8.

[21]Hymns on Faith XIV.5 (English translation in *The Harp of
the Spirit*, no. 1; in the second edition half the first line has unfortunately fallen out).

[22]*Demonstration* XVIII.10. One might compare the allegorical
interpretation given by Philo of Alexandria, *On the Allegorical
Laws* II.491, where the man represents the *nous* or intellect, the

his father and his mother and cleaves to his wife," Aphrahat asks "What father and mother does he leave when he takes a wife? The sense is this: as long as a man has not yet taken a wife, he loves and honors God his Father and the Holy Spirit his Mother; but when a person takes a wife, he leaves his Father and Mother—in the sense indicated just now—and his mind is caught up with this world, and his mind, heart and thought are drawn away from God to the world."

It seems clear that in certain circles of the early Syrian Church the view was held that only the "single"—whether *bthule*, "virgins," or married *qaddishe*—could enter the eschatological Bridal Chamber. Such an attitude is above all reflected in the early encratite work known as the Acts of Thomas.[23]

---

father and mother divine Wisdom and Virtue, and the wife sensuality. Ephrem, however, gives a quite different interpretation to this verse in his Commentary on Genesis.

[23]In section 12, for example, Thomas urges a newly wed couple to abstain from marital union in the following words: "Realize that as soon as you preserve yourselves from this filthy intercourse, you will become pure temples. . . . You will wait in hope for the true Wedding Feast . . . and you will be numbered with those who enter the Bridal Chamber." The Acts of Thomas are usually dated to the third century: they were written in Syriac, but an early Greek translation also survives. Very much the same idea is to be found in the second-century Gospel of Thomas, Logion 75: "Many are standing at the door, but 'the single' [*monachoi*] are the ones who will enter the Bridal Chamber"; *monachos* is of course used here in its pre-monastic sense of "single, celibate" (a good discussion of the development of the term will be found in F. Morard, "Monachos, Moine: histoire du terme grec jusqu'au IVe siècle," *Freiburger Zeitschrift für Philosophie und Theologie* 20 (1973), pp. 332-411). It should be stressed that both Aphrahat and Ephrem have a more balanced view of the role of marriage than that found in the Acts of Thomas. The imagery of the Bridal Chamber (very popular in Ephrem) is found in many Greek writers as well, e.g. *Saint John Climacus, The Ladder of Divine Ascent* (Holy Transfiguration Monastery, Brookline, 1978), Step 2.9, "No one will

The parable which provides the starting point for much of this imagery, that of the Wise and Foolish Virgins, also introduces a second motif that is of great importance, that of "wakefulness." Early Syriac writers generally follow the usage of the author of the Book of Daniel and refer to angelic beings as "Wakers" or "Watchers," and so to the Syriac reader the wise virgins in the parable are associated with a characteristic of the angelic life, and it is precisely the marriageless nature of the angelic life that provides further motivation for the ideal of virginity. Here a key passage is to be found in St Luke's Gospel; he, alone of the three Evangelists who record this dominical saying, speaks of the marriageless life of angels as something to be anticipated already on earth. The Old Syriac Gospels, translated below, make this idea even more prominent than does the original Greek text (Luke 20:35-6):

Those who have become worthy to receive that world [the Kingdom] and that Resurrection from the dead do not marry, nor can they die, for they have been made equal with the angels.

That the ascetic life is an angelic life, *angelikos bios,* was to become a commonplace in subsequent monastic literature. Here, however, only one further facet of this particular ideal may be noted: Aphrahat associates the need to become an "alien," a "stranger" to the world,[24] both with the angelic life and with the imitation of Christ (the significance of this aspect will emerge later).

The third basis lying behind the ideal of virginity rested on the theme of St Ephrem's hymn cycle translated in this

enter the Heavenly bride chamber wearing a crown unless he makes the first, second and third renunciation."

[24]*Demonstration* VI.1 (English translation in *Select Library of Nicene Fathers,* series II, vol. 13; the title, "On the members of the Covenant," is there misleadingly translated "On monks").

book, the Paradise narrative. Baptism is regularly understood by the early Syriac Fathers (and of course many
others) as a re-entry into Paradise,[25] an eschatological
Paradise even more glorious than the primordial Paradise
of the Genesis narrative. Now these writers were quick to
observe that, according to the biblical text, Adam and Eve
had marital intercourse only after their expulsion from
Paradise (Genesis 4:1); they therefore deduced that sexual
abstinence was a characteristic of marital life in Paradise
and therefore also among members of the Church, which
ideally anticipates the eschatological Paradise.

Adam's "singleness" in Paradise in fact brings us back
to the starting point of this diversion from our discussion
of the ideal of the *iḥidaya*, for there is evidence, both in
Jewish and in Christian sources, that Adam himself was
sometimes described as being *iḥidaya*. In Genesis 3:22,
where the Hebrew text (followed by the Septuagint and
Peshitta) has "Behold, Adam has become[26] like one of us,
knowing good and evil," the Palestinian Targum tradition
introduces the term *iḥidaya*, using it both of Adam and of
God: "Behold, the first Adam whom I created is single
[*iḥiday*] in the world, just as I am single [*iḥiday*] in the
heights of heaven." Although the term *iḥidaya* does not
appear in the Syriac translation of Genesis 1-3, it is an
epithet applied to Adam in the Wisdom of Solomon 10:1:
"It was Wisdom which preserved the ancestral father, the
iḥidaya ["single" or "unique"], who had been created in
the world."

Although it is unlikely in the extreme that St Ephrem
knew the Palestinian Targum directly, it is quite possible
that he was aware of this strand of Jewish exegesis, whose

---

[25]This idea is expressed most notably in the imagery of the Robe
of Glory, lost at the Fall and regained at Baptism (see below).

[26]The Hebrew and the Syriac Peshitta could also be understood
in the sense "Adam was . . ."

importance lay in the association of the "singleness" of
Adam with the singleness of God, using precisely the term
ihidaya, so central to Syriac "proto-monasticism." Now in
the Syriac New Testament the term *Monogenes*, "Only-
Begotten," is regularly translated as *ihida* or *ihidaya*, and
so we have exactly the same term employed in Syriac and
in Jewish Aramaic for both God and man. Clearly, then,
among the various associations behind the Syriac term
ihidaya used of those living an ascetic life, that of follower
of Christ the *Ihidaya* par excellence will be very prominent.
Indeed, to a Syriac speaker, the individual *ihidaya* will be
to Christ (the *Ihidaya*) what the individual Christian
(*mshihaya*) is to Christ (*Mshiha*). This is brought out in
one of the Epiphany hymns (VIII.16) attributed to St
Ephrem:

> See, people being baptized and becoming "virgins"
> and *qaddishe*, having gone down to the font, have
> been baptized in it and put on the single *Ihidaya*,

based on St Paul's metaphor of "putting on Christ" at
baptism (Galatians 3:27).

Putting on Christ the *Ihidaya*, and becoming an *ihidaya*
oneself, was seen not just as an outward adoption of the
name, but as a radical reorientation of one's life involving
the "putting on," the imitation, of the whole of Christ's
own life: in order to share in His resurrection it is necessary to participate in His sufferings as well. Thus the
Christian life is inevitably one of "afflictions," which will
take on quite different forms with different individuals; but
at the same time, as Aphrahat says,[27] "the *Ihidaya* from
the bosom of His Father gives joy to all *ihidaye*."

With all this in mind we can begin to see that the key
term, *ihidaya*, lying behind the early Syriac ascetic ideal

---

[27]*Demonstration* VI.6.

to which St Ephrem witnesses, was exceedingly rich in its connotations (and for that reason I have frequently left it untranslated in the discussion above): "single, celibate, singular, single-minded, follower of Christ the *Iḥidaya* (Only-Begotten)." It is extremely likely that St Ephrem himself was an *iḥidaya*; in any case, it is with the proto-monasticism centered on the ideals lying behind this term, rather that with the Egyptian monasticism which eventually spread to Syria, that St Ephrem should be associated. No doubt the various resonances that lie behind this term are reflected in the following final stanza to a hymn on Prayer and Faith, where St Ephrem is clearly alluding to himself (Hymns on Faith, XX.17):

> Let prayer within wipe clean the murky thoughts,
> let faith wipe clean the senses outwardly,
> and let one such man who is divided
> collect himself together and become one before You.

St Ephrem's Writings

St Ephrem was a prolific writer[28]; over four hundred of his hymns come down to us, and quite a number more are known to have existed once but are now lost. He was also the author of verse homilies and several prose works; the latter include both treatises against various heretical writers and biblical commentaries. Whereas the polemical works are today chiefly of antiquarian interest, the commentaries contain many profound insights; of the extant Old Testament commentaries that on Genesis is the most important, and since this provides a helpful backdrop to *The Hymns on Paradise,* a translation of the section covering Genesis

---

[28]For a list of St Ephrem's main writings, see the Bibliographical Note.

2-3 is provided at the end of the translation of the hymn cycle. Most accessible (in every sense of the word) of Ephrem's commentaries is that on the Diatessaron, or Harmony of the Four Gospels; until recently this was only known in an early Armenian translation, but in 1956 the Syriac original of at least part of the work was rediscovered, and subsequently a French translation of the entire commentary (which contains several passages of great lyrical beauty) has become available in *Sources Chrétiennes* (no. 121). The other New Testament commentaries, on the Acts of the Apostles and on the Pauline Epistles, survive only in Armenian translation (a situation which also applies to some of the hymns and verse homilies). Standing halfway between the prose and the poetry come two works in artistic prose, one a comparatively extensive work entitled "On Our Lord," the other, in the form of a letter addressed to a certain Publius, being a meditation, of considerable profundity, on the Last Judgment.

St Ephrem's reputation as a writer was very great both in the Syriac and in the Graeco-Latin world. Anonymous and spurious works, however, have a strong tendency to become attached to famous names, and it is now known that a large number of works attributed to St Ephrem are certainly not by him, and nowhere does this apply so much as to the body of writings in Greek and Latin which are transmitted under his name. Between the definitely genuine and the definitely spurious comes a rather large number of works, especially verse homilies (*memre*), whose status is at present doubtful or disputed.

Most important among the clearly genuine writings are the great hymn cycles, such as the Paradise hymns translated here. It is upon these lyric poems (*madrashe*), with their highly imaginative use of imagery and great sensitivity and artistry in the use of language as well as the profundity of their thought, that St Ephrem's reputation as a poet of outstanding stature stands.

These cycles, of varying extent, reach us in a number of sixth-century manuscripts under titles which often refer only to a small group (usually the first) within that cycle. Thus, for example, only the first half of the Nisibene hymns have anything to do with the town of Nisibis; the remainder almost all have to do with the theme of Christ's descent into the underworld Sheol. The most extensive of these cycles are entitled On Faith (with 87 hymns), On Nisibis (77 hymns), Against Heresies (56 hymns), On Virginity (52 hymns), On the Church (52 hymns), and On the Nativity (28 hymns); smaller cycles include On Paradise (15 hymns), On Lent (10 hymns) and On the Paschal Season (three separate groups, in all 35 hymns). The collection of the hymns into these cycles must go back at least to the late fifth century, but whether they represent Ephrem's own arrangement or not is uncertain: this may well be the case with the smaller collections, such as that on Paradise,[29] but is much less likely with larger cycles.

Later on, especially from the eighth and ninth centuries onward, copyists tended to abbreviate the hymns; about this time, too, selections were made from Ephrem's hymns for inclusion in the vast festal hymnaries designed to cover the whole ecclesiastical year. The compilers of these would frequently reduce the number of stanzas of a hymn which they chose to include, and over the years this process of reduction would be continued by copyists with the sad result (reflected in the printed editions) that the train of thought is sometimes seriously distorted.[30]

---

[29]One of the three sixth-century manuscripts containing this cycle states that the cycle finishes at the end of XII.15 (evidently incorrectly). Hymns XIII and XIV form an alphabetic acrostic.

[30]In contrast to the extensive use made of some hymn cycles (notably those on the Nativity and Pascha) in the seven-volume Mosul edition of the *Fenqitho* (1886-96), the Paradise hymns are hardly used at all: a single stanza, VI.19, is incorporated into a *madrasha* in Vol. VI, p. 638, and the opening of hymn X appears

We know from an index of St Ephrem's hymns preserved in a sixth- or seventh-century manuscript in the Monastery of St Catherine on Mount Sinai that there were once in circulation considerably more of St Ephrem's hymns than today survive, though a few of these poems are available at one remove, in Armenian translation.

Translations of Ephrem's works into Greek (and probably also Latin) were already being made at an early date, as we learn from both Jerome and Sozomen. It so happens that there comes down to us a vast number of texts in Greek, Slavonic and Latin which are attributed to St Ephrem, but of these only a small proportion can lay any claim to being genuine, and in many cases they are not even translations from Syriac at all. This, however, is an area where a great deal of sorting and critical analysis still remains to be done. The same also applies to the extensive translations of works attributed to Ephrem into oriental languages, above all Arabic.

Poetic Form

St Ephrem's poetry falls into two different categories, the *memre* or verse homilies, written in couplets of 7+7 syllables, and the *madrashe* or hymns in stanza form, where all the stanzas of a particular hymn will be constructed on a single syllabic pattern chosen out of the great many syllabic patterns available. As far as we can tell Syriac poetry was from the first based on syllabic principles, and this certainly applies both to an excerpt quoted by Mara, son of Serapion, who may be a late first-century pagan writer, and to the two archaic poems, both in six-syllable couplets, incorporated into the Acts of Thomas, the Hymn

to have served as the model for another *madrasha,* in vol. III, p. 359.

of the Bride of Light and the Hymn of the Pearl. We know from Ephrem's own hymns that both Bardaisan (who died in 222) and Mani (who died in c. 276) already wrote *madrashe,*[31] but even without this information, the extremely sophisticated use of the *madrasha* verse form exemplified in St Ephrem's poetry would require us to postulate a long prehistory for this genre.

In Sozomen's and Theodoret's notices of Ephrem's life, however, we have seen that quite a different picture is given: according to Sozomen, Syriac verse form was an innovation, inspired by Greek models, made by Harmonius, a reputed son of Bardaisan. This picture fails to ring true for two main reasons: first, Syriac syllabic verse form was certainly already in existence before the time of Harmonius (whose very existence is in fact a matter of some doubt); second, if syllabic verse form had been taken over by Harmonius from Greek, it would have been at a time when syllabic verse (as opposed to classical quantitative verse) was only just making its first appearances in the Greek world—definitely before it had had time to gain sufficient prestige to warrant its wholesale transfer to another linguistic milieu. What, then, are we to make of Sozomen's claim? It would appear that both he and Theodoret simply witness to the general lack of appreciation, common among Greek writers in antiquity, of the culture of "barbarian" (non-Greek) nations. Sozomen and Theodoret, faced with the undisputed prestige of Ephrem as a Syriac poet, deduced that "barbarian" Syriac could only have achieved such heights of poetic excellence under the influence and inspiration of Greek models.

In his *madrashe,* which form the major part of his

---

[31]Hymns against Heresies I.16 (Mani) and LIII.5 (Bardaisan). Relics of Manichaean hymnography survive in Coptic (edited by C. R. C. Allberry) and in various Iranian dialects (edited by M. Boyce).

poetic output, St Ephrem employs some fifty or so different stanza patterns, ranging from the very simple (such as 5+4+5+4 syllables) to the highly complex. As the *madrashe* were sung, the manuscripts transmitting them normally give the title of their melody, called the *qala*, consisting of the first words of a particular *madrasha* using that stanza pattern. In several cases we have more than one *qala* attested for a single stanza pattern, but this does not necessarily imply that there were several different melodies. Since Syriac scribes (apart from a few Melkite scribes on Mt Sinai) never adopted any notational system for writing down the music, the original melodies to which the *madrashe* were sung are lost.

Whereas most hymn cycles exhibit a whole variety of different stanza patterns, that on Paradise employ only one, with a *qala* which was later regularly entitled *Pardaisa*, after the cycle.[32] The syllabic pattern for each stanza is as follows: 5+5. 5+5. 5+5. 7. 5+5. 5+5. Rhyme is never present except for special effect (and this is only rare). Whether there was also a regular stress pattern, corresponding to the homotony of the Byzantine kontakion, as well as the syllabic pattern, is very uncertain. A transcription of a single stanza (I.4) will illustrate the syllabic structure of Ephrem's verse:

> *b-aynā d-re'yānā   hzītheh l-pardaysā*
> *w-rawmē d-kull tūrīn   sīmīn thēt rawmeh*
> *l-'eqbaw mtā balhud   rīsheh d-māmōlā*

---

[32]In the manuscripts of Ephrem's own hymn cycles this particular stanza pattern is actually given five different *qālā* titles; most manuscripts of the Paradise cycle name the *qālā* as *dīnā d-sharbāthā*, rather than *pardaisā*. In some other of Ephrem's hymns employing the same metrical pattern the *qālā* title is given as *bayya b-mulkānē*, the opening words of the seventh of the Hymns on Paradise (thus Hymns on Faith XXXI, XXXIX-XLVIII; Nativity III; Nisibene Hymns II-III, XLIII-XLIX).

l-reglaw nshaq wa-sged w-ethpnī
d-nessaq ndush rīshā d-tūrē w-rāmāthā.
'eqbaw d-haw nāsheq w-rīshā d-kull qāphah.

A literal translation of this would be:

with-the-eye of-the-mind   I-beheld Paradise
and-the-heights of-all mountains
    are-placed beneath its-height.
To-its-heels there-reached alone
    the-summit of-the-flood,
its-feet did-it-kiss and-worship and-turn-back
in-order-to-go-up (and) trample the-summit
    of-mountains and-hills:
the-heels of-the-former does-it-kiss
    and-the-summit of-everything (else) does-it-buffet.

St Ephrem's Theological Vision

St Ephrem's poetry is profoundly theological in character, expressing his awareness of the sacramental character
of the created world, and of the potential of everything in
the created world to act as a witness and pointer to the
Creator. Everything is imbued with significance, but, although this meaning is objectively present (St Ephrem calls
it "the hidden power," or "meaning," *ḥayla kasya*), it
requires the eye of faith on the part of each individual to
penetrate both inward and beyond the outer material
reality in order to perceive the relationship, sacramental in
character, between the exterior physical and interior spiritual realm. By positing this inherent link between the
material and spiritual worlds St Ephrem is thus very far
removed from those Christian writers who, usually under
Neoplatonic influence, tend to denigrate the value of the
material world.

Since it is inevitable that any human perception of this "hidden power," this objective spiritual reality, will be of a subjective character, varying from individual to individual, poetry proves a far more satisfactory vehicle for expressing this experience than does prose, for poetry is able to preserve a fluidity and dynamism which eschews the use of all definitions, seeing that these, by their inherently static character, are apt to have a fossilizing effect on any theological enquiry.

St Ephrem's mode of theological discussion, essentially Biblical and Semitic in character, thus stands in sharp contrast to the dogmatizing approach which, under the influence of Hellenic philosophy, has characterized much of the Christian theology with which we are today familiar. Indeed it is precisely because Ephrem's theology is not tied to a particular cultural or philosophical background, but rather operates by means of imagery and symbolism which are basic to all human experience, that his theological vision, as expressed in his hymns, has a freshness and immediacy today that few other theological works from the early Christian period can hope to achieve.

The difference between these two approaches, Hellenic and Semitic, can be well illustrated if one visualizes a circle with a point in the center, where the point represents the object of theological enquiry; the philosophical tradition of theology will seek to define, to set *horoi*, "boundaries" or "definitions," to this central point, whereas St Ephrem's Semitic approach through his poetry will provide a series of paradoxical statements situated as it were at opposite points on the circumference of the circle: the central point is left undefined, but something of its nature can be inferred by joining up the various opposite points around the circumference. St Ephrem is always very insistent that, since the center point representing the aspect of God's being under discussion stands outside creation, it thus lies beyond the ability of the created intellect to comprehend—and any claim to be able to do so is blasphemous. In all this St Ephrem is obviously very much in harmony with the apophatic tradition of later Greek theology.

The ontological gap between God the Creator and his creation is in fact impassable as far as any created being is concerned, and any knowledge of, or statement about, God would be impossible had not God himself taken the initiative and bridged this chasm. He does this by a variety of different means, each manifesting something of his hiddenness. The mode of his self-revelation is essentially threefold: by means of types and symbols which are operative in both Nature and in Scripture, by allowing Himself— the indescribable—to be described in Scripture in human terms and language, and then, supremely, by actually becoming part of the created world, at the Incarnation.

Types and Symbols

On a number of occasions St Ephrem speaks of the natural world and the Bible as God's two witnesses; in the Paradise hymns (V.2) we have the following statement:

In his book Moses described
    the creation of the natural world,
so that both Nature and Scripture
    might bear witness to the Creator:
Nature, through man's use of it,
    Scripture, through his reading it;
they are the witnesses
    which reach everywhere,
they are to be found at all times,
    present at every hour,
confuting the unbeliever
    who defames the Creator.

Nature and Scripture testify to God by means of the symbols and types which they contain, for these act as pointers to spiritual reality or "truth" (*shrara*). St Ephrem uses a variety of different terms more or less interchangeably, but the most important of these is *raza*, "mystery" (but often best translated "symbol"). The word, of Persian origin, first appears in Daniel where its primary meaning is that of "secret"; subsequently it occurs in the texts of the Qumran community, and very probably it is the Semitic term lying behind St Paul's use of the word *mysterion*. By St Ephrem's time *raza* had taken on a wide variety of different connotations, and in the present context it is significant that the plural, *raze,* like the Greek *mysteria,* refers to the liturgical "Mysteries." As a typological term *raza,* "symbol," indicates the connection between two different modes of reality, and here it is important to remember that the Fathers employ the term "symbol" in a strong sense, quite different from that of modern usage: for them a symbol actually participates in some sense with the spiritual reality it symbolizes, whereas for most people today the term "symbol" tends to imply something essentially different from the thing it symbolizes. The Patristic view, of course, accords much greater significance to the symbol, whereas modern usage plays down the value of the symbol. Clearly this difference greatly affects St Ephrem's attitude toward the material world.

Types and symbols are a means of expressing relationships and connections, of instilling meaning into everything. They operate in several different ways, between the Old Testament and the New, between this world and the heavenly, between the New Testament and the Sacraments, between the Sacraments and the eschaton. In every case they "reveal" something of what is otherwise "hidden."

The dynamic tension implied behind St Ephrem's use of these two terms, "hidden" and "revealed," is of great importance in the structure of his thought, and his handling of it can at times be quite complex. Basically, the opposition between these two poles can be seen to operate in two different ways. On what we may call the objective plane, "hiddenness" (*kasyutha*) is something characteristic of the *raze*, both in the sense of "symbols" (whether in Nature or in Scripture) and in the sense of "Sacraments"; in the former case these symbols represent a hidden state of what is to be revealed in Christ, whose Incarnation provides the key to unlocking the treasure-store of symbols; in the latter case, the Sacraments represent in a hidden way what will be fully revealed at the end of time in Paradise. In both cases what is revealed (*galyutha*) represents an objective reality, but one which can only be experienced in this life in a subjective and hidden way.

The second way of looking at this opposition between "hidden" and "revealed" is to begin from the subjective viewpoint of humanity. Under this schema the term *kasyutha*, "hiddenness," refers to God, knowledge of whom would have been totally inaccessible to created human beings had he not first revealed aspects of himself to his creation. Thus, within time, the reality of the Incarnation is hidden as far as the Old Testament writers are concerned, and the glimpses they have of this reality, expressed as *raze* or "symbols" in the Biblical writings of the Old Covenant, have been made possible for them only because God has "revealed" Himself in some respect there. Likewise, in the Sacraments God has revealed something of a hidden objective reality which will only be fully revealed outside time and space, in Paradise.

It is significant that when St Ephrem is employing this second, subjective way of looking at things, he does not use the abstract noun *galyutha* to denote what is revealed, but the plural *galyatha*, "things revealed," thus emphasizing that he is only talking about a partial revelation. In the hands of his poetic genius the interplay between these two ways of using the terms "hidden" and "revealed" can often be highly subtle.

It will be found that throughout all his works St Ephrem lays a great deal of emphasis on the hiddenness of God. The reason for this is not hard to discern, for St Ephrem was living at a time when Arianism in its various forms was posing a serious threat to the Orthodox Church. The Arians, by locating the Generation of the Son in time, not only placed the Logos in a position subordinate to the Father, but also situated him on our side, as it were, of the ontological gap between created and Creator. And if the Logos is part of creation, then everything about Him could potentially be grasped and described by the human intellect, a fellow child of creation. To St Ephrem and to the Orthodox this was of course a double blasphemy, and it is against the logical consequence of the initial assumption that St Ephrem is constantly at pains to argue. Since for him the eternal Generation of the Son from the Father lay outside time, and belonged to the far side of the ontological chasm between created and Creator, then any attempt to use the created intellect in order to try to penetrate the "hiddenness" of this mystery was both presumptuous and totally misguided.

St Ephrem's recurring polemic against the misuse of the human intellect in matters of theology can give the initial impression that he is anti-intellectual in his approach; this, however, is far from the case, for the intellect is to him an extremely important gift of God to humanity, but, if it is to be used properly, it must not vainly seek to understand things which lie beyond its comprehension. In other words, the area of the intellect's activity necessarily lies within the created world—where indeed there is ample scope for it. The matter is put succinctly in one of the hymns on Faith (VIII.9).

There *is* intellectual enquiry in the Church,
investigating what is revealed:
the intellect was *not* intended to pry into hidden things.

The Garment of Words

Since the human mind is part of creation, it is unable
of its own accord to leap across this gap between created
and Creator and to provide any description at all of the
hidden Godhead. No theology, talking about God, would
in fact be possible at all but for God's own initiative and
condescension: stirred by love for humanity, the culmination of His creative activity, He Himself has crossed this
gap and allowed Himself to be described in human language
and in human terms in the Scriptures as part of the process
of His self-revelation. God thus "put on names"—the
metaphors used of him in the Bible—and in this way the
human intellect is provided with a whole variety of pointers
upward, hinting at various aspects of the hiddenness of
God, whose true nature, however, cannot possibly be described by, or contained in, human language.

This "incarnation" of God into human language is perhaps most fully described by St Ephrem in the thirty-first
hymn in the collection On Faith, whose opening five stanzas
are worth quoting in full:

1. Let us give thanks to God
      who clothed Himself in the names of the body's
      various parts:
   Scriptures refers to His "ears"
      to teach us that He listens to us;
   it speaks of His "eyes,"
      to show that He sees us.
   It was just the names of such things
      that He put on,

and—although in His true being
  there is no wrath or regret—
yet He put on these names
  because of our weakness.

Response: Blessed is He who has appeared to our
          human race under so many metaphors.

2. We should realize that,
      had He not put on the names
    of such things,
      it would not have been possible for Him
    to speak with us humans.
      By means of what belongs to us did He draw
      close to us:
    He clothed Himself in language,
      so that He might clothe us
    in His mode of life.
      He asked for our form and put this on,
    and then, as a father with his children,
      He spoke with our childish state.

3. It is our metaphors that He put on—
      though He did not literally do so;
    He then took them off—without actually doing so:
      when wearing them, He was at the same time
      stripped of them.
    He puts on one when it is beneficial,
      then strips it off in exchange for another;
    the fact that He strips off
      and puts on all sorts of metaphors
    tells us that the metaphor
      does not apply to His true Being:
    because that Being is hidden,
      He has depicted it by means of what is visible.

4. In one place He was like an Old Man
    and the Ancient of Days,
  then again, He became like a Hero,
    a valiant Warrior.
  For the purposes of judgment He was an Old Man,
    but for conflict He was Valiant.
  In one place He was delaying;
    elsewhere, having run,
  He became weary.
    In one place He was asleep,
  in another, in need:
      by every means did He weary Himself so as to
      gain us.

5. For this is the Good One,
    who could have forced us to please Him,
  without any trouble to Himself;
    but instead He toiled by every means
  so that we might act pleasingly to Him of our own
  free will,
    that we might depict our beauty
  with the colors
    that our own free will had gathered;
  whereas, if He had adorned us,
    then we would have resembled
  a portrait that someone else had painted,
    adorning it with his own colors.

(St Ephrem humorously goes on to compare God's action in teaching humanity about Himself to that of someone who tries to teach a parrot to talk, with the help of a mirror.)

St Ephrem stresses that we, on our part, must not abuse God's condescension by taking these metaphors literally— that would be to misunderstand Biblical language totally. Any purely literal interpretation of Scripture is therefore to

be rejected, and this is a point to which Ephrem returns
on a number of occasions, but perhaps most forcefully in
stanzas 6 and 7 of the eleventh hymn on Paradise:

> If someone concentrates his attention solely
>   on the metaphors used of God's majesty,
> he abuses and misrepresents that majesty,
>   and thus errs
> by means of those metaphors
>   with which God had clothed Himself for his benefit,
> and he is ungrateful to that Grace
>   which stooped low
> to the level of his childishness:
>   although it has nothing in common with him,
> yet Grace clothed itself in his likeness
>   in order to bring him to the likeness of itself.
>
> Do not let your intellect
>   be disturbed by mere names,
> for Paradise has simply clothed itself
>   in terms that are akin to you;
> it is not because it is impoverished
>   that it put on your imagery;
> rather, your nature is far too weak
>   to be able
> to attain to its greatness,
>   and its beauties are much diminished
> by being depicted in the pale colors
>   with which you are familiar.

There exists, in Ephrem's thought, an important parallel-
ism between God's two "incarnations," his "putting on
metaphors" and his "putting on the body": in both cases
it is essential to penetrate beyond what is seen outwardly
—the literal meaning of the Biblical text and the humanity
of Christ—in order to reach any proper understanding of

the significance of these two "incarnations." Just as, by concentrating solely on the humanity of Christ, one would fail to perceive anything of His divinity, so too, by fixing one's sole attention on the literal meaning of the Biblical text, one will remain blind to its inner, spiritual, meaning.[33] Conversely, a total disregard for the literal meaning of the text would itself also lead one to an unbalanced view of Scripture, just as any any failure to take account of the humanity of Christ would result in a completely misguided view of Christology. Any true understanding of Scripture accordingly needs to preserve a proper balance: the literal meaning of the Biblical text has its own validity, but at the same time the text has an inner meaning (the "hidden power" in Ephrem's terminology) which belongs to a different mode of reality.

St Ephrem's Concept of Paradise

A literal reading of the Biblical text would leave one with the impression that Paradise is a concept which belongs only to the beginnings of creation. In the religious climate of the centuries at the turn of the Christian era, however, a much richer understanding of Paradise had grown up within Judaism, finding expression in apocalyptic works such as the First Book on Enoch (perhaps of the second century BC); in these writings Paradise is understood as representing both the primordial and the eschatological state at the end of time, for it has now also become the abode of the righteous.[34]

---

[33]This analogy between the two "incarnations" incidentally helps to explain why the Fathers frequently speak of a purely literal understanding of Scripture as a Jewish characteristic.

[34]Enoch 61:12; a similar idea is found in the Jewish Palestinian Targum tradition at Genesis 3:24: "He drove out Adam. Now He had caused the Glory of His Shekhina (Divine Presence) to dwell above the Garden of Eden from the very beginning, between

The location of this Paradise (envisaged, as we shall see, as a mountain) was variously expressed. Some writers, taking Genesis 2:8 ("And the Lord God planted a garden—Paradise in the Septuagint—in Eden, in the East") as their cue, held it to be on the eastern extremities of this earth, while according to others Paradise represented the eschatological transfiguration of the Promised Land, where the Paradise mountain was equated with the new Jerusalem, situated on Mount Sion. More significant, from the point of view of St Ephrem's conception of Paradise, is an interpretation given to Genesis 2:8 which is to be found both in the Peshitta, the Syriac translation of the Bible, and in the Targumim, the Jewish Aramaic versions which often reflect current exegesis in synagogue circles: whereas the Septuagint (followed by all the standard modern translations) renders the Hebrew *miqqedem* as "to the East," the Peshitta and the two Targum traditions, Palestinian and Babylonian, take the word as having temporal, rather than spatial, reference, "from the beginning," that is, belonging to primordial or sacred time. This is made clearest in Targum pseudo-Jonathan, which, although it belongs to the early Islamic period in its present form, nevertheless contains some old traditions. Here the verse is expanded so as to include the eschatological role of Paradise:

A garden had been planted in Eden for the just by the Word of the Lord God before the creation of the world, and He made Adam reside there once He had created him.

It was to views of this sort that early Christian writers were heirs, and, just as there was evidently a considerable

---

the Cherubim. . . . He created the Law and established the Garden of Eden for the righteous, so that they might eat from it and enjoy its fruits, seeing that they had kept the commandments of the Law in this world" (Fragment Targum).

variety of opinions floating around within Judaism, so too
a number of different conceptual pictures of Paradise are
to be found in Christian writers. Some locate the Paradise
of Genesis on earth and regard it as a place different from
the eschatological Paradise, to which they accord only an
intermediary role, a stepping stone as it were, for the souls
of the just awaiting the Resurrection at the end of time.
This view, found in a variety of different forms, makes a
sharp functional distinction between Paradise and the
Kingdom of Heaven, and it claimed to find support for this
in Luke 23:43, where the penitent thief is told by Christ,
"This day you shall be with me in Paradise."

Quite a different view, clearly rooted in late Judaism,
held the primordial and eschatological Paradise to be the
same, and to represent the definitive place of beatitude after
the final Resurrection. In an unsophisticated form such
a Paradise could be located on this earth, but among more
thoughtful writers (among whom are both St Ephrem and
St Gregory of Nyssa) this Paradise was not to be situated
in time or space; rather, it belonged to a different order of
reality.

With these preliminaries we may now turn to the details
of St Ephrem's understanding of Paradise.

St Ephrem, like Dante many centuries later, envisaged
Paradise as a mountain. Although the Genesis narrative
itself has nothing to suggest this, there are hints elsewhere
in the Old Testament which point to such a conception,
notably in Ezekiel 28:13-14, where "Eden, the Garden
[Paradise] of God" is described as "the holy mountain of
God." The prophet makes use here of an idea, well attested
throughout the ancient Near East, of a cosmic mountain
upon which the deity resided (elsewhere in the Old Testament this holy mountain is sometimes identified with Sion,
as in Psalm 47(48):1-2). Jewish literature of the inter-
testamental period indicates that by that time the concept
of Paradise as a mountain was a widespread one. As a

matter of fact a hint of it is even introduced into the Syriac
translation of Genesis 4:8, where Cain says to Abel "Let
us go to the *valley*" (Septuagint and other versions have
"plain" or "field"): in his Commentary on Genesis St
Ephrem deduces from this that they were still at that time
on higher ground, in other words the foothills of the Paradise mountain from which their parents had been expelled.[35]

Since early Syriac Christianity clearly had many direct
and indirect links with contemporary Judaism, it is no sur-
prise that St Ephrem should have taken over this particular
concept of Paradise as well.

The Paradise Hymns provide us with a number of topographical details which, taken together, can give us some
idea of how St Ephrem conceptualized this Paradisiacal
mountain. We learn that the mountain is circular (I.8) and
that it encircles the "Great Sea" (II.6), enclosing both land
and sea (I.8-9). The Flood reached only its foothills (I.4),
and on these foothills is situated the "fence" or "barrier"
(*syaga*), guarded by the Cherub with the revolving sword
(II.7, IV.1, based on Genesis 3:24). This fence demarcates
the lowest extremity of Paradise. Halfway up is the Tree
of Knowledge which provides an internal boundary beyond
and higher than which Adam and Eve were forbidden to
go (III.3); this Tree acts as a sanctuary curtain hiding
the Holy of Holies, which is the Tree of Life higher up
(III.2). On the summit of the mountain resides the Divine
Presence, the Shekhina (Syriac *shkinta*).

This Paradise mountain is also understood as consisting
of three concentric circles which divide the mountain up

---

[35]Commentary on Genesis III.5: "From the fact that he said,
'Let us travel to the valley,' it can be deduced that either they were
living on the lower mountain slopes of Paradise, and that he led
him down to the valley; or that Abel was shepherding his sheep
on the mountain, and Cain went up to bring him down to the
valley." Compare R. Murray, *Symbols of Church and Kingdom*,
Cambridge 1975), pp. 306-10.

into three separate levels, reserved for different categories of the blessed. These levels at the same time correspond to the various levels in the Ark and on Mount Sinai (II.10-13).

The Tree of Knowledge and the Tree of Life are, as we have already seen, described respectively as the "sanctuary curtain or veil" (III.5, 13, compare XV.8; Syriac *appay tar'a*) and the "inner sanctuary" or "Holy of Holies" (III.5, 14; Syriac *qdush qudshe*); in other words, Paradise also represents both the Temple and its Christian successor, the Church (St Ephrem would have put it the other way around: the Old Testament Temple and the Christian Church here on earth are both pale reflections of Paradise). This is not all, for the threefold structure of the human person (IX.20), consisting of intellectual spirit (*tar'itha*), soul (*naphsha*) and body (*gushma*), also reflects the divisions of Paradise. Drawing all this together we can outline St Ephrem's conception of Paradise as follows in diagrammatic form:

	Paradise	*Ark*	*Sinai*	*Human person*
summit: (*risha*)	Shekhina		the Glorious One	divinity
	Tree of Life (Holy of Holies)			
heights: (*rawma*)	the glorious (*nassihe*)	Noah	Moses	intellectual spirit
	Tree of Knowledge (Sanctuary Veil)			
slopes (*gabbe*)	the just (*zaddiqe*)	birds	Aaron	soul
	the Fence (*syaga*)		priests	
lower slopes: (*shphule*)	the repentant (*tayyabe*)	animals	people	body

It would appear, then, that St Ephrem visualized Paradise as a conically shaped mountain whose base circumference encircles the "Great Sea," or Okeanos, which itself was thought to surround the earth. Our sky will thus be formed by the inside of the conical mountain of Paradise, a concept very similar to that described by St Gregory of Nyssa.[36] Paradise thus both transcends and envelops the world.

The fact that such a model is illogical in terms of our (and Ephrem's) experience of the world should warn us to pay attention to St Ephrem's statement that the terrestrial terms used for Paradise should not be taken literally (II.4-5) and to avert us at once to his real intention: he is deliberately drawing our attention to the distinction between sacred space (and time) and ordinary space (and time). Paradise belongs to the former, our world to the latter; they represent two different orders of reality and modes of existence. As Jean Daniélou put it:[37] "C'est ce que nous appelons cosmologie mythique ou les dimensions ont valeur ontologique et non scientifique, sans cesser d'être réelles."

By locating Paradise outside time and space as we know them, Ephrem was deliberately going against some much more literalist views of Paradise that were current in the early Christian period; thus in the second century Theophilus of Antioch deduces from the Biblical words "God planted Paradise in Eden to the east" and "He caused to come up from the earth every tree which was beautiful to see and good to eat" that "the divine Scripture clearly teaches us that Paradise is under this very heaven under which are the East and the earth" (*To Autolycus*, II.24). In the early fifth century Theodore of Mopsuestia was like-

---

[36]See for example *Patrologia Graeca* 44, col. 1209A (On the Beatitudes, 2).

[37]"Terre et Paradis chez les Pères de l'Église," *Eranos Jahrbuch* 22 (1953), p. 451.

wise to interpret the Biblical text in a similarly literalist way. St Ephrem's understanding (which he shares above all with St Gregory of Nyssa) would seem to be far more profound and much richer in meaning; furthermore, precisely because he locates Paradise outside geographical space, his views are left unaffected by modern advances in scientific knowledge.

Since primordial Paradise belongs outside time and space it also serves as the eschatological Paradise, the home of the righteous and glorious after the final Resurrection. Indeed, the saints already in this life anticipate the life of Paradise:

> The assembly of saints
>   bears resemblance to Paradise:
> in it each day is plucked
>   the fruit of Him who gives life to all (VI.8);

and

> Among the saints none is naked,
>   for they have put on glory;
> nor is any clad in those leaves
>   or standing in shame,
> for they have found, through our Lord,
>   the robe that belongs to Adam and Eve (VI.9).

Nevertheless, St Ephrem is emphatic that this eschatological Paradise can only be entered in the resurrected state of the body; in one hymn (V.7-10) his pragmatic mind is concerned with the possibility of overcrowded conditions in Paradise; the difficulty is resolved, however, when he discovers from various scriptural passages that the resurrected body is of a different nature from the physical. Nor can the soul alone enter Paradise: it must be accompanied by the resurrected body (VIII.9). This explains why, in his vision of Paradise, Ephrem expects the Garden to be empty (V.II), seeing that the final Resurrection has not yet taken place.

Since this Resurrection was regarded as occurring not just outside time, but also at the end of time, it was necessary to provide some accompanying concept to explain what happened to the departed between physical death and the final Resurrection. Here, once again, St Ephrem and other early Syriac writers took over another idea of Jewish origin, that of "the sleep of the dead in Sheol," a period of unconscious existence which bridges the gap between death and the Resurrection, between historical and sacred time. According to this view, judgment is usually understood as taking place only at the final Resurrection, when the "sheep" and the "goats" are separated off, to the right and to the left (Matthew 25:33); it is only then that the just may enter Paradise, while the wicked undergo "second death"[38] as they are relegated to Gehenna.

In a few passages St Ephrem hesitatingly speculates about the possibility of some sort of intermediary position for repentant sinners:

Blessed the sinner
   who has received mercy there
and is deemed worthy to be given access
   to the environs of Paradise:
even though he remains outside,
   he may pasture there through grace.

---

[38]Although this term occurs in the Revelation of St John (e.g. 2:11), early Syriac writers will have borrowed it directly or indirectly from Jewish sources, seeing that the Revelation was not part of the early Syriac canon of the New Testament and no translation of it into Syriac was made till the late fifth or sixth century. In Jewish writings the phrase occurs chiefly in the Targums (for details see "Jewish traditions in Syriac sources," *Journal of Jewish Studies* 30 (1979), pp. 220-1).

> As I reflected I was fearful again
>   because I had presumed
> to suppose that there might be
>   between the Garden and Hell's fire
> a place where those who have found mercy
>   can receive chastisement and forgiveness (X:14,
>   compare I.16).

Indeed, in Ephrem's tripartite schema of Paradise, the place allocated to the "penitent" would appear to be outside the "fence" provided by the Cherub, even though this is never explicitly stated. Perhaps, however, the problem is unreal, in that the "barrier" is in fact removed by the Cross and so the boundary on the lower slopes of Paradise can be understood as having been extended downwards to include the "low ground" allocated to the "penitent" immediately below; some support for such a view might be claimed from the Syriac translation of Ephesians 2:14 which reads [Christ] dismantled the barrier [*syaga*] which stood in the midst." (See further below, p. 63.)

The Two Trees

It has already been seen that the two Trees, of Life and of Knowledge, have different positions on the Paradise mountain, the former corresponding to the Holy of Holies, the latter to the sanctuary veil. The Tree of Knowledge is thus the "gate" leading to the Tree of Life (III.13).

St Ephrem, in common with a number of other early Christian writers, held the view that God created Adam and Eve in an intermediate state: if they kept the commandment not to eat the fruit of the Tree of Knowledge, then they would be rewarded by being allowed to eat it and would thereby be enabled to progress to the Tree of

Life,[39] thus acquiring divinity (as we shall see). In the
event, however, their unthinking greed led them to break
the commandment, and although they did thereby gain
knowledge, it was only a knowledge of what they had lost
by their disobedience. In one of the Hymns on the Fast
(III.3) St Ephrem puts it as follows

Who is there who can expound that Tree
   which caused those who sought it to go astray?
It is an invisible target, hidden from the eyes,
   which wearies those who shoot at it.
It is both the Tree of Knowledge, and of the opposite;
   it is the cause of knowledge, for by it humanity knows
what was the gift that was lost
   and the punishment that took its place.
Blessed is that Fruit which has mingled
   a knowledge of the Tree of Life into mortals.

The knowledge imparted by the Tree of Knowledge is
of an objective nature, but this knowledge can be experienced subjectively in totally different ways, depending on
the attitude of the person who partakes of it. This extremely
important insight is explored especially in the third of the
Paradise hymns.

---

[39]A very similar idea is found in the Palestinian Targum tradition
at Genesis 3:22: "And the Lord God said: 'Behold the First
Adam, whom I created unique [ihiday] in the world, just as I am
unique in the highest heavens. From him shall many peoples arise,
and from him shall one people arise which knows how to distinguish between Good and Evil. Had he [Adam] kept the precepts
of the Law and observed its commandment, he would have lived
and existed like the Tree of Life forever; but now that he has failed
to keep the precepts of the Law and has not observed its commandment, We shall drive him out of the Garden of Eden, before he
stretches out his hand to take of the Tree of Life, eats it and lives
on forever," (Neofiti). A similar view, described as Jewish, is out-
lined by Nemesius, *On the nature of man, 5.*

In the Commentary on Genesis St Ephrem asks himself why God did not from the very first grant to Adam and Eve the higher state he had intended for them. His answer is again of great importance and illustrates the very prominent role which he allocates to human free will (*ḥerutha,* literally "freedom"):[40]

Now because God had given to Adam everything inside and outside Paradise through Grace, requiring nothing in return, either for his creation or for the glory in which He had clothed him, He nevertheless, out of Justice,[41] held back one tree from him to whom He had given, in Grace, everything in Paradise and on earth, in the air and in the seas. For when God created Adam, He did not make him mortal, nor did He fashion him as immortal; this was so that Adam himself, either through keeping the commandment, or by transgressing it, might acquire from this one of the trees whichever outcome he wanted . . . Even though God had given them everything else out of Grace, He wished to confer on them, out of Justice, the immortal life which is granted through eating of the Tree of Life. He therefore laid down this commandment. Not that it was a large commandment, commensurate with the superlative reward that was in preparation for them; no, He only withheld from them a single tree, just so that they might be subject to a commandment. But He gave them the whole of

---

[40]Commentary on Genesis II.17.

[41]Stanzas 9-10 of the third hymn of the Paradise cycle make a very similar point. St Ephrem is very fond of balancing the two divine attributes of Grace and Justice against each other; one might compare the use of the terms *middat ha-din* and *middat ha-rahamim,* "aspects of Judgment and of Mercy," in Rabbinic literature.

Paradise, so that they would not feel any compulsion
to transgress the law.

In their intermediate state Adam and Eve are not even
aware of the existence of the Tree of Life higher up the
mountain of Paradise, for the Tree of Knowledge serves as
a sanctuary curtain, veiling the Holy of Holies from sight
(III.13,17). St Ephrem gives two main reasons for God's
action in keeping the Tree of Life hidden from their sight:
first, so that the vision of its beauty might be reserved as
a reward for them if they kept the commandment (III.9),
and second, so that the attraction of its surpassing beauty
might not make the temptation to eat the forbidden fruit,
in the hopes of reaching it, irresistible. This second point
is made notably in the Commentary on Genesis (II.17),
where he adds a further reason.

> God had created the Tree of Life and hidden it from
> Adam and Eve, first, so that it should not, with its
> beauty, stir up conflict with them and so double their
> struggle, and also because it was inappropriate that
> they should be observant of the commandment of
> Him who cannot be seen for the sake of a reward that
> was there before their eyes.

Under the Old Covenant the Tree of Life continued to
remain hidden from humanity, and it was only with the
Crucifixion that it was finally made manifest.

> Greatly saddened was the Tree of Life
> when it beheld Adam stolen away from it;
> it sank down into the virgin ground and was hidden
> —to burst forth and reappear on Golgotha;
> humanity, like birds that are chased,
> took refuge in it
> so that it might return them to their proper home.

The chaser was chased away, while the doves
that had been chased
now hop with joy in Paradise.

(Hymn on Virginity XVI.10)

As the source of immortality, "the Tree of Life is the symbol of the Son of the Living One" (Hymn on the Church XLIX.16), whose Eucharistic fruit is plucked daily in the Church, as we learn from the seventh of the Paradise hymns (Stanza 8):

The assembly of saints
has a semblance of Paradise:
in it, daily, is plucked the Fruit
of Him who gives life to all.

More frequently, however, St Ephrem prefers to dwell on the typological contrast between the Tree of Knowledge, whose fruit brought death to Adam, and the Tree of the Cross, whose fruit restores life to humanity:

In His love there came to us the blessed Tree:
the one wood undid the work of the other,
the one fruit was annulled by the other,
that which brought death by that which is alive.

(Hymn on Virginity VIII.1).

A similar contrast is found in the Commentary on the Diatessaron (XXI.25): "we have eaten his Body instead of the fruit of the Tree." In one of the hymns preserved only in Armenian translation (XLIX.9-10) we find a rather different emphasis, for here Christ is contrasted with the Tree of Life:

With the blade of the sword of the cherub
was the path to the Tree of Life shut off,

but to the Peoples has the Lord of that Tree
    given Himself as food.

Whereas Eden's other trees were provided
    for that former Adam to eat,
for us the very Planter of the Garden
    has become the food for our souls.

The following verse,

Whereas we had left that Garden
    along with Adam, as he left it behind,
now that the sword has been removed by the lance,
    we may return there,

where Genesis 3:24 is contrasted with John 19:34, provides
a convenient introduction to our next topic.

The Fence and the Sword

Originally God's commandment had sufficed to prevent
Adam and Eve from penetrating too far up the sacred
mountain, but their disobedience led to the imposition of
an inviolate boundary provided by the cherub with the
sharp revolving sword (Gen. 3:24):

The Just One saw how Adam had become audacious
    because He had been lenient
and knew that he would overstep again
    if He continued thus:
Adam trampled down
    that gentle and pleasant boundary,
so instead God made for Adam
    a boundary guarded by force.

> The mere words of the commandment
>   had been the boundary to the Tree,
> but now the cherub and a sharp sword
>   provided the fence to Paradise.
>
> (Hymn on Paradise IV.1)

This more permanent boundary was situated at a point lower down the mountain, by the fig trees with whose leaves Adam and Eve had clothed themselves (Hymn II.7). It is on the low ground, beyond this lower circumference, that the primordial pair take up their residence after their expulsion from the Garden (I.10).

As we have already seen in passing, this new boundary imposed after the Fall is termed the "fence" or "barrier" (*syaga*) by St Ephrem. The word is derived in early Syriac tradition from Ephesians 2:14, which reads in the standard Syriac version of the New Testament, the Peshitta, as follows: "Christ . . . dismantled the barrier [*syaga*] which stood in the midst, and the enmity, in his flesh; and the law with the commandments He has annulled by His own commandments." In the Greek original the barrier (*phragmos*) probably refers to the Law, but the Syriac translator has so phrased the sentence that the "barrier" and the "law" could readily be taken as referring to two different things, and this is how early Syriac writers regularly understand the passage, for they link the "barrier" of Ephesians with the Fall; justification for this interpretation was found in St Paul's mention of the "enmity" which Syriac writers saw as a reference to Genesis 3:15, "I will place enmity between you and the woman." Thus in the Book of Steps[42] (a collection of homilies on the spiritual life compiled around AD 400) the Pauline passage is paraphrased with the words ". . . breach the barrier of enmity which existed because of the transgression of the commandment." Aphra-

---

[42]*Homily* XV.12 (in *Patrologia Syriaca* III).

hat too, who was writing before Ephrem, in the second quarter of the fourth century, is already using the term *syaga*, "barrier," "fence," in connection with Genesis 3:24, when he speaks[43] of the Tree of Life as being "*fenced in* at the command of the Almighty by the fearsome sword and the encircling flame"; elsewhere[44] his phraseology explicitly links Gen. 3:24 with Eph. 2:14: "Christ broke down the fence and the blade of the sword."

The precise moment at which Christ effected the dismantling of this fence was when his own side was pierced by the lance on the Cross (John 19:34): "The sword that pierced Christ removed the sword guarding Paradise," states St Ephrem in one of the Hymns on the Crucifixion (IX.2), while in the Hymns on the Nativity (VIII.4) he writes:

Blessed be the Merciful One
who saw the sword beside Paradise,
barring the way to the Tree of Life;
He came and took to Himself a body
which was wounded so that,
by the opening of His side,
He might open up the way into Paradise.

John 19:34 is a key verse for St Ephrem's symbolic theology, seeing that it serves as a focal point for a great deal of his typological exegesis.[45] The lance and the side of Christ, the Second Adam, both point back to the Genesis

---

[43]*Demonstration* XXIII.3 (in *Patrologia Syriaca* II).

[44]*Demonstration* XIV.31 (in *Patrologia Syriaca* I).

[45]On this theme see R. Murray, "The Lance which re-opened Paradise," *Orientalia Christiana Periodica* 39 (1973), pp. 224-34, 491; S. P. Brock, "The Mysteries hidden in the side of Christ," *Sobornost* VIII.6 (1978), pp. 462-72; *The Holy Spirit in the Syrian Baptismal Tradition*, pp. 88-93, and *The Luminous Eye*, pp. 61-4.

narrative, to the cherub's sword[46] and to the First Adam's side which gave miraculous birth to Eve. The side of Christ, whence issue—or flow[47]—water and blood, also looks forward to the Sacraments of Baptism and the Eucharist, and, at the same time, to the equally miraculous birth of the Church. Two passages from St Ephrem's Commentary on the Diatessaron (Gospel Harmony) illustrate this line of interpretation. In one we have a straightforward exposition:

"There came forth blood and water": that is, His Church, which is build on his "side." Just as in the case of Adam, his wife was taken from his side. Adam's wife is his "rib," so our Lord's "blood" is His Church. From Adam's rib issued death, from our Lord's rib, life.

(Commentary on the Diatessaron XXI.11)

The other passage, however, takes on a lyrical character:

I ran to all Your limbs, and from them all I received every kind of gift. Through the side pierced with the sword I entered the Garden fenced in with the sword. Let us enter in through that side which was pierced, since we were stripped naked by the counsel of the

---

[46]Although the Biblical texts of Gen 3:24 and John 19:34 employ two different words, Syriac writers, in order to emphasize the typological connections, frequently use the same word with reference to both weapons.

[47]In allusions to the passage the wording is sometimes deliberately altered from "issued" to "flowed" in order to link this passage with a christological interpretation of John 7:37-8, depending on a different punctuation from that which has become traditional, thus: "If anyone thirsts, let everyone who believes in me come to me and drink: as the Scripture has said, 'Out of His belly shall *flow* rivers of living water'"; compare R. Murray, *Symbols of Church and Kingdom*, p. 213.

rib that was extracted. The fire that burned in Adam,
burned him in that rib of his. For this reason the side
of the Second Adam has been pierced, and from it
comes a flow of water to quench the fire of the first
Adam.

(Commentary on the Diatessaron XXI.10)

The Robe of Glory

One thing that will quickly strike the modern reader is
St Ephrem's predilection for clothing imagery[48]: at the Fall
Adam and Eve are stripped of a "Robe of Glory," God
"puts on names" in the Scriptures, Christ "puts on the
body" at the Incarnation,[49] He "puts on our weakness."
In all this St Ephrem is simply developing imagery which
is already present in abundance in both the Old and the
New Testaments; particularly important in this connection
are passages in St Paul's writings, such as Romans 13:14
and Galatians 3:27, where the Christian is said to "put
on Christ." St Ephrem is by no means the first writer to
exploit this metaphor, for it is to be met with in almost
all early Christian writers, and its application to the Incarnation is already found in Melito and other early Christian authors; his originality, however, lies in the way in
which he employs this imagery as a means of linking
together in a dynamic fashion the whole of salvation his-

---

[48]See A. Kowalski, " 'Rivestiti di gloria.' Adamo ed Eva nel
commento di S. Efrem a Gen 2, 25," *Cristianesimo nella storia*
(Bologna) 3 (1982), pp. 41-60; S. P. Brock, "Clothing metaphors
as a means of theological expression in Syriac tradition," in M.
Schmidt (ed.), *Typus, Symbol, Allegorie bei den östlichen Vätern
und ihren Parallelen im Mittelalter* (*Eichstätter Beiträge* 4, 1982),
pp. 11-40, and *The Luminous Eye*, ch. 5.

[49]This phrase features in the oldest Syriac translation of the
Nicene Creed, representing *sarkōthenta* in the Greek.

tory; it is a means of indicating the interrelatedness between every stage in this continuing working out of divine Providence. Basically there are four main episodes which go to make up this cosmic drama: at the Fall, Adam and Eve lose the "Robe of Glory" with which they had originally been clothed in Paradise; in order to re-clothe the naked Adam and Eve (in other words, humanity), God himself "puts on the body" from Mary, and at the Baptism Christ laid the Robe of Glory in the river Jordan, making it available once again for humanity to put on at baptism; then, at his or her baptism, the individual Christian, in "putting on Christ," puts on the Robe of Glory, thus re-entering the terrestrial anticipation of the eschatological Paradise, in other words, the Church; finally, at the Resurrection of the Dead, the just will in all reality reenter the celestial Paradise, clothed in their Robes of Glory.

The Robe of Glory thus provides the thread which links up between the primordial and the eschatological Paradise, and the mention of it in any one context is intended immediately to conjure up in the reader's mind the entire span of salvation history, thus admirably emphasizing, for example, the place of each individual Christian's Baptism within the divine economy as a whole.

Whence does the term "Robe of Glory" originate? It is evident that St Ephrem and the other early Syriac writers derived it ultimately from Jewish circles, where the term arose from a particular interpretation of Genesis 3:21.[50] In that verse the Hebrew and the ancient versions read, "And the Lord God made for Adam and his wife garments of skin"; it so happens, however, that the Hebrew word for "skin" is very similar to that for "light," and a famous late-first-century rabbi, Rabbi Meir, is reputed to have had a manuscript of Genesis which actually read "garments of

---

[50]For details see the literature cited in the articles mentioned in note 48. See also the note to Commentary on Genesis II.33.

light." The Aramaic Targum tradition, furthermore, trans-
lates the phrase by "garments of honor (*or* glory)," very
similar to the "Robe of Glory," characteristic of Syriac
writers. Now although Genesis 3:21 is usually understood
as referring to the time *after* the Fall, there was clearly a
tradition current in some Jewish circles around the turn
of the Christian era which understood it to refer to the time
prior to the Fall: "the Lord God *had* made . . . garments
of glory." Syriac writers themselves appear never to have
interpreted the time reference in Genesis 3:21 in this way,
but it must be from circles that once did that they have
derived the term "Robe of Glory."[51] It is interesting that
the idea of this original Robe of Glory worn by Adam
seems to have been already familiar to the Syriac translator
of Psalm 8:6, which he rendered "You created man a little
less than the angels: in honor and glory did you *clothe*
him" (both the Hebrew and the Greek have ". . . did you
crown him").

In the Hymns on Paradise St Ephrem alludes to Adam's
loss of his original Robe of Glory a number of times,
notably in XV.8-9, but for the subsequent history of this
Robe and its restoration we have to turn for the most part
to other works. In the Hymns on Virginity (XVI.9) the
whole purpose of the Incarnation is seen as the restoration
of Adam's original garment.

> Christ came to find Adam who had gone astray,
> to return him to Eden in the garment of light.

In order to restore Adam to the glory of which he had been
stripped at the Fall, God the Word likewise has to strip
himself of his divine glory and "put on Adam's body." The

---

[51]The terms "robe" or "garment of light," reflecting R. Meir's
Biblical text, are also often used by Syriac writers (in the Paradise
hymns see VII.5, IX.28 and XIV.8).

symmetry between the Fall and the Restoration is brought out in one of the Nativity hymns (XXIII.13).

> All these changes did the Merciful One make,
> stripping off glory and putting on a body;
> for He had devised a way to reclothe Adam
> in that glory which he had stripped off.
> He was wrapped in swaddling clothes,
> corresponding to Adam's leaves,
> He put on clothes
> in place of Adam's skins;
> He was baptized for Adam's sin,
> He was embalmed for Adam's death,
> He rose and raised Adam up in His glory.
> Blessed is He who descended,
> put Adam on and ascended.

A somewhat different slant is to be found in the Commentary on the Diatessaron (XVI.10), where St Ephrem sees the episode of the withering of the fig tree (Matthew 21:20-21) as pointing to the replacement of the fig leaves of Genesis 3:7 by the Robe of Glory, recovered for Adam and Eve by Christ:

> When Adam sinned and was stripped of the glory in which he had been clothed, he covered his nakedness with fig leaves. Our Savior came and underwent suffering in order to heal Adam's wounds and provide a garment of glory for his nakedness. He dried up the fig tree, in order to show that there would no longer be any need of fig leaves to serve as Adam's garment, since Adam had returned to his former glory, and so no longer had any need of leaves or garments of skin.

And elsewhere Ephrem exclaims (Hymn on the Fast II.2),

"Blessed is He who had pity on Adam's leaves, and sent a
Robe of Glory to cover his naked state."

In all this it is characteristic of St Ephrem's essentially
Semitic understanding of the Biblical narrative that he is
able to move rapidly to and fro between the individual and
the collective, between Adam and humanity as a whole.
Thus Christ is said to have "put on Adam" (Hymn on the
Fast II.4), "Adam's body" (Nisibene Hymn XXXV.8),
"humanity" (Hymn on the Fast III.6), and "our body"
(Hymn on the Nativity XXII.39). Quite often some refer-
ence to the Virgin will be incorporated, as in one of the
Nativity hymns (IV.188):

> She wove Him a garment and clothed Him
> because He had stripped off His glory.

Later writers, such as Jacob of Serugh, relate how Christ
"came to Baptism, went down and placed in the baptismal
water the Robe of Glory, to be there for Adam, who had
lost it."[52] Although St Ephrem does not have such explicit
references to this aspect of the Robe imagery, it is certainly
implied in a number of passages such as the following from
the Hymns on the Church (XXXVI.6):

> The brightness which Moses put on[53]
> was wrapped on him from without,
> whereas the river in which Christ was baptized
> put on Light from within,
> and so did Mary's body, in which He resided,
> gleam from within.

That Christian baptism was the means for the recovery of

---

[52]Homily 94, On Faith (ed. P. Bedjan, III, p. 593).

[53]Exodus 34:29 (Sinai). A translation of the entire hymn will
be found in *Eastern Churches Review* 7 (1975), pp. 137-44.

the lost Robe is made clear from one of the Epiphany hymns attributed to St Ephrem (XII.4):

Instead of with leaves from the trees
He clothed them with glory in the water.

In several passages the Robe of Glory takes on an eschatological aspect, as in the Paradise hymn VI.9:

Among the saints
   their nakedness is clothed with glory,
none is clad with leaves
   or stands ashamed,
for they have found, through our Lord,
   the robe that belongs to Adam and Eve.

In one of a famous group of poems (Hymn on Faith LXXXIII.2) on the symbolism of the pearl, St Ephrem addresses the pearl as follows:

You are like Eve,
who though naked was still clothed.
Cursed is he who deceived and left her stripped.
The serpent cannot strip off your glory;
in Eden women shall be clothed in light, resembling you.

This garment of glory or light is also identified as the wedding garment of the parable in Matthew 22:12, and with this in mind St Ephrem exhorts the baptized to preserve their robe unspotted in readiness for the eschatological banquet:

The Firstborn wrapped himself in a body
as a veil to hide His glory.
The immortal Bride shines out in that robe;
let the guests in their robes resemble Him in His.

Let your bodies—which are your clothing—shine out,
for they bound in fetters that man whose body was
   stained.
O whiten my stains at Your banquet with your radiance.
(Nisibene Hymn XLIII.21)

In a fine meditation on the Last Judgment, where he gazes
on "the mirror of the Gospel," St Ephrem moves from the
wedding feast to the theme of Paradise as the actual bridal
chamber:[54]

I saw there beautiful people, and I was desirous of
their beauty and I saw the place of the good where
they were standing, and I was eager for their position.
I saw their bridal chamber opposite, which no one
who has not a lamp may enter; I saw their joy, and
I myself sat down in mourning, not possessing works
worthy of that bridal chamber. I saw them clothed
with the Robe of Light, and I was grieved that I had
prepared no virtuous raiment.

Paradise Regained: Divinization

The ultimate aim of the Incarnation, however, was not
just to restore Adam's humanity to Paradise, but to raise
humanity to the position of honor that Adam and Eve
would have been granted had they kept the divine commandment, as St Ephrem explains in the Commentary on
Genesis II.23.

. . . had the serpent been rejected, along with the sin,
they would have eaten of the Tree of Life, and the

---

[54]Letter to Publius, 12 (ed. with English translation in *Le Muséon*
89 (1976), p. 284). For the significance of the "Bridal chamber,"
see above, on St Ephrem and monasticism.

Tree of Knowledge would not have been withheld
from them any longer; from the one they would have
acquired infallible knowledge, and from the other
they would have received immortal life. They would
have acquired divinity [*allahutha*] in humanity; and
had they thus acquired infallible knowledge and immortal life, they would have done so in this body.

Elsewhere, in one of the Nisibene hymns (LXIX.12)[55] he
puts the matter succinctly as follows:

The Most High knew that Adam wanted to become a
   god,
so He sent His Son who put him on in order to grant
   him his desire.

The same idea recurs in the Hymns on Virginity (XLVIII.
17-18):

Divinity flew down and descended
to raise and draw up humanity.
The Son has made beautiful the servant's deformity,
and he has become a god, just as he desired.

It has sometimes been said that the concept of the divinization, or *theosis,* of humanity is something that crept into
Christianity, and especially Eastern Christianity, under
Hellenic influence. It is clear, however, that St Ephrem,
whom Theodoret described as "unacquainted with the language of the Greeks,"[56] and whose thought patterns are
essentially Semitic and Biblical in character, is nonetheless
an important witness to this teaching. Moreover in this
context it should be recalled that, since the term "son of"

---

[55]A translation of the whole hymn is to be found in *The Harp
of the Spirit,* no. 16.

[56]Ecclesiastical History IV.29. On divinization see also *The
Luminous Eye,* pp. 123-7.

implies "belonging to the category of," the title "children of God" to which Christians attain at Baptism would suggest to the Semitic mind that they had, potentially, the characteristics of divine beings, in other words, immortality. Once again the theological content of St Ephrem's poetry is remarkably similar to that of his Greek contemporaries—only the mode of expression is different. Just as St Athanasius expressed this mystery epigrammatically ("God became man so that man might become God"), so too, in his own way, did St Ephrem:

> He gave us divinity,
> we gave Him humanity
> (Hymn on Faith V.17)

The Present Translation

St Ephrem's hymns present the translator with many problems arising out of the condensed and allusive style of his writing. At times his thought requires considerable unpacking if it is to become meaningful to the modern reader, and in such places (where any literal translation would actually prove misleading) a slightly expanded translation has been given. Sometimes it has also proved necessary to resort to the use of an explanatory note as well, but, in order not to divert the reader unduly from the text, these notes are collected together at the end of the translation. An asterisk in the text alerts the reader to these notes.

In the case of Biblical references and allusions, however, it has seemed preferable to give these (or at least the most important of them) in the form of footnotes to the translation. Here it should be observed that St Ephrem is extremely fond of evoking an entire Biblical passage by means of the use of a single choice word, and clearly he expected his hearers to know the Bible extremely well; a good example of this can be found in the various allusions to Matthew 15:27 where the Canaanite woman replies to Christ "Yes, Lord, yet even the dogs eat the crumbs that fall from their master's table" (Hymns I.16, VII.26 and IX.29).

In his use of imagery Ephrem is often highly original, and at times his choice can strike the modern reader as somewhat bizarre; in such cases the translator might be tempted to alter the imagery, but as far as possible I have tried to avoid this. A further difficulty lies in the fact that certain Syriac words and their standard English equivalents can have entirely different ranges of meaning. Perhaps no term is more problematic than *'ubba*, "womb," for in Syriac the word, a favorite of Ephrem's, can also mean "lap," "bosom," "bud," "cavity," "pocket," "gulf," etc. Since Ephrem uses the term in a whole variety of different senses the translator is forced by the varying contexts to employ several English renderings, thereby losing an important linking element in St Ephrem's symbolic thought pattern.

A modern translation of St Ephrem's poetry thus needs to steer a narrow course between the Scylla of pedantic literalism and the Charybdis of excessive freedom, for either extreme can prove positively misleading. Although the present rendering has aimed at sailing such a course, it certainly would not presume to claim to have escaped unscathed from any encounter with the rocks on either side, but if it be judged at least to have avoided total shipwreck, then this is thanks to the skill and sensitivity of Elizabeth Rapp and Dana Miller[57] who carefully worked over and greatly improved drafts of the translation.

Sebastian Brock

---

[57]Dana Miller also generously gave me his own draft translation of Hymns I-IX; I have greatly benefited from his insights into the meaning of several obscure passages.

2.

THE HYMNS ON PARADISE

HYMN I

At the outset, St Ephrem emphasizes that the Biblical narrative concerning Paradise in Genesis 2-3 contains much more profound teaching than any literal reading of the text would suggest. Our reading of it should accordingly be accompanied by a sense both of awe and of love; only then will the "inner vision" be enabled to perceive something of the profundity of its meaning.

The second half of the poem concerns the topographical relationship of Paradise to the fallen world—first in the context of Adam and his immediate descendants, and then from an eschatological point of view, based on the parable of Lazarus and the Rich Man (Luke 16:19-31).

1. Moses, who instructs all men
        with his celestial writings,
    He, the master* of the Hebrews,
        has instructed us in his teaching—
    the Law,* which constitutes
        a very treasure house of revelations,
    wherein is revealed
        the tale of the Garden—
    described by things visible,
        but glorious for what lies hidden,

*See notes at end of translation.

spoken of in few words,
    yet wondrous with its many plants.

RESPONSE: Praise to Your righteousness
             which exalts those who prove victorious.

2. I took my stand halfway
    between awe and love;
a yearning for Paradise
    invited me to explore it,
but awe at its majesty
    restrained me from my search.
With wisdom, however,
    I reconciled the two;
I revered what lay hidden
    and meditated on what was revealed.
The aim of my search was to gain profit,
    the aim of my silence was to find succor.

3. Joyfully did I embark
    on the tale of Paradise—
a tale that is short to read
    but rich to explore.
My tongue read the story's
    outward narrative,
while my intellect took wing
    and soared upward in awe
as it perceived the splendor of Paradise—
    not indeed as it really is,
but insofar as humanity
    is granted to comprehend it.

4. With the eye of my mind
    I gazed upon Paradise;
the summit of every mountain
    is lower than its summit,

the crest of the Flood
  reached only its foothills;[1]
these it kissed with reverence
  before turning back
to rise above and subdue the peak
  of every hill and mountain.
The foothills of Paradise it kisses,
  while every summit it buffets.

5. Not that the ascent to Paradise
     is arduous because of its height,
   for those who inherit it
     experience no toil there.
   With its beauty it joyfully
     urges on those who ascend.
   Amidst glorious rays
     it lies resplendent,
   all fragrant with its scents;
     magnificent clouds
   fashion the abodes
     of those who are worthy of it.

6. From their abodes
     the children of light descend,
   they rejoice in the midst of the world
     where they had been persecuted;
   they dance on the sea's surface
     and do not sink,
   for Simon, although a "Rock,"
     did not sink.[2]
   Blessed is he who has seen,
     together with them, his beloved ones,

---

[1]Gen. 7:19.
[2]Matt. 14:29.

below in their bands of disciples,
   and on high in their bridal chambers.*

7. The clouds, their chariots
   fly through the air;
each of them has become the leader
   of those he has taught;[3]
his chariot corresponds to his labors,
   his glory corresponds to his followers.[4]
Blessed the person who has seen
   as they fly
the Prophets with their bands,
   the Apostles with their multitudes;
for whoever has both acted and taught
   is great in the Kingdom.[5]

8. But because the sight of Paradise
   is far removed,
and the eye's range
   cannot attain to it,
I have described it over simply,
   making bold a little.
Resembling that halo
   which surrounds the moon
we should look upon Paradise
   as being circular too,
having both sea and dry land
   encompassed within it.

9. And because my tongue overflows
   as one who has sucked
the sweetness of Paradise,
   I will portray it in diverse forms.

---

[3]Dan. 12:3.
[4]cf 1 Cor. 3:8.
[5]Matt. 5:19.

Moses made a crown
   for that resplendent altar;[6]
with a wreath entirely of gold
   did he crown
the altar in its beauty.
   Thus gloriously entwined
is the wreath of Paradise
   that encircles the whole of creation.

10. When Adam sinned
      God cast him forth from Paradise,
    but in His grace He granted him
      the low ground beyond it,
    settling him in the valley*
      below the foothills of Paradise;
    but when mankind even there continued to sin
      they were blotted out,
    and because they were unworthy
      to be neighbors of Paradise,
    God commanded the Ark
      to cast them out on Mount Qardu.*[7]

11. There the families
      of the two brothers had separated:
    Cain went off by himself
      and lived in the land of Nod,[8]
    a place lower still
      than that of Sheth and Enosh;
    but those who lived on higher ground,
      who were called
    "the children of God,"*[9]
      left their own region and came down

---

[6]Exod. 30:3.
[7]Gen. 8:4 (Peshitta).
[8]Gen. 4:16.
[9]Gen. 6:2.

to take wives
from the daughters of Cain down below.

12. The children of light
dwell on the heights of Paradise,
and beyond the Abyss
they espy the rich man;[10]
he too, as he raises his eyes,
beholds Lazarus,
and calls out to Abraham
to have pity on him.
But Abraham, that man so full of pity,
who even had pity on Sodom,[11]
has no pity yonder
for him who showed no pity.

13. The Abyss severs any love
which might act as a mediary,
thus preventing the love of the just
from being bound to the wicked,
so that the good should not be tortured
by the sight, in Gehenna,
of their children or brothers
or family—
a mother,* who had denied Christ,
imploring mercy from her son
or her maid or her daughter,
who all had suffered affliction for the sake of
Christ's teaching.

14. There the persecuted laugh
at their persecutors,

---

[10]Luke 16:26.
[11]Gen. 8:20.

the afflicted at those who had caused them affliction,
    the slain at those who had put them to death,
the Prophets at those who had stoned them,
    the Apostles at those who had crucified them.
The children of light reside
    in their lofty abode
and, as they gaze on the wicked
    and count their evil actions,
they are amazed to what extent these people
    have cut off all hope by committing such iniquity.

15. Woe to him who tries to hide
        his shameful deeds in the dark,
    who does wrong and then tries to deceive
        those who have seen;
    having gone in and committed some wrong
        he lies so as to deceive those who have heard.
    May the wings of Your grace[12]
        protect me,
    for there the accusing finger
        points out
    and daily proclaims
        the sinner's shame and hidden dealings.

16. What I have told
        must suffice my boldness;
    but if there is anyone
        who dares to go on and say
    "As for the dull-witted and simple people,
        who have done wrong out of ignorance,
    once they have been punished
        and paid their debt,
    He who is good allows them to dwell
        in some remote corner of Paradise

---

[12]Ps. 16(17):8.

where they can graze on
    that blessed food of 'the crumbs' . . ."[13]*

17. This place, despised and spurned
        by the denizens of Paradise,
    those who burn in Gehenna
        hungrily desire;
    their torment doubles
        at the sight of its fountains,
    they quiver violently
        as they stand on the opposite side;
    the rich man, too, begs for succor,*
        but there is no one to wet his tongue,[14]
    for fire is within them,
        while the water is opposite them.

HYMN II

At Judgment the gate to Paradise will sift the good from the
bad; its discerning powers allow in all those who, while still
on earth, have forged a key to Paradise by the conduct of their
lives whereas those who have neglected to do so find them-
selved excluded: their moral ugliness is incompatible with the
spiritual beauties of Paradise. Those who prove worthy of
Paradise will be given an abode appropriate to the character
of their life on earth; like the Ark and like Mount Sinai at
the Lawgiving, Paradise is divided into three different levels.

1. Blessed is he
        for whom Paradise yearns.
    Yes, Paradise yearns for the man whose goodness
    makes him beautiful;

---

[13]Matt. 15:27 and parallels.
[14]Luke 16:24.

it engulfs him at its gateway,
it embraces him in its bosom,
    it caresses him in its very womb;
for it splits open and receives him
    into its inmost parts.
But if there is someone it abhors,
    it removes him and casts him out;
this is the gate of testing
    that belongs to Him who loves mankind.[1]

RESPONSE: Blessed is He who was pierced
            and so removed the sword from the entry to
            Paradise.*[2]

2. Forge here on earth and take
        the key* to Paradise;
    the Door that welcomes you[3]
        smiles radiantly upon you;
    the Door, all discerning,
        conforms its measure to those who enter it:
    in its wisdom
        it shrinks and it grows.
    According to the stature and rank
        attained by each person,
    it shows by its dimensions
        whether they are perfect, or lacking in something.

3. When people see
        that they have lost everything,
    that riches do not endure
        and carnal desires no longer exist,

[1]cf John 10:7.
[2]Gen. 3:24; John 19:34.
[3]cf John 10:9.

that beauty and power
  disappear and vanish,
then they recollect themselves
  and are filled with remorse,
because, choked with care,
  they heard with contempt those words,
"Your possessions are but a passing dream,
  your inheritance, darkness."*

4. What they once possessed they have lost,
    and found what they never had;
  they desired happiness, but it flew away,
    and the woe they had dreaded has arrived;
  what they had hoped on has proved an illusion,
      and what they never sought for they have now
      found.
  They groan because they are brought low
    and have been "robbed,"
  for their way of life deceived them,
    while their torment is very real;
  their luxurious living* has vanished,
    and their punishment does not come to an end.

5. The righteous, too, perceive
    that their own affliction no longer exists,
  their suffering does not endure,
    their burden no longer remains,
  and it seems as if no anguish
    had ever assailed them.
  Their fasts appear
    as though a mere dream,
  for they have woken as it were from sleep
    to discover Paradise
  and the Kingdom's table[4]
    spread out before them.

4Luke 22:30.

6. By those who are outside
    the summit cannot be scaled,
   but from inside Paradise inclines its whole self
    to all who ascend it;
   the whole of its interior
    gazes upon the just with joy.
   Paradise girds the loins
    of the world,
   encircling the great sea;
    neighbor to the beings on high,
   friendly to those within it,
    hostile to those without.

7. At its boundary I saw
    figs, growing in a sheltered place,[5]
   from which crowns were made that adorned
    the brows of the guilty pair,
   while their leaves blushed, as it were,
    for him who was stripped naked:
   their leaves were required for those two
    who had lost their garments;*
   although they covered Adam,
    still they made him blush with shame and repent,
   because, in a place of such splendor,
    a man who is naked is filled with shame.

8. Who is capable of gazing
    upon the Garden's splendor,
   seeing how glorious it is in all its design,
    how harmonious in its proportions,
   how spacious for those who dwell there,
    how radiant with its abodes?
   Its fountains delight
    with their fragrance,

[5]Gen. 3:7.

but when they issue forth toward us*
    they become impoverished in our country,
since they put on the savors
    of our land as we drink them.

9. Indeed, that Will
        for whom everything is easy
    constrains these abundant
        fountains of Paradise,
    confining them with land,
        like water channels;
    He summoned them to issue forth
        in our direction,
    just as He bound up the waters[6]
        in the bosom of His clouds,
    ready to be sent forth into the atmosphere
        at the bidding of His Will.

10. When He made this intricate design
        He varied its beauties,
    so that some levels
        were far more glorious than others.
    To the degree that one level
        is higher than another,
    so too is its glory
        the more sublime.
    In this way He allots
        the foothills to the most lowly,
    the slopes to those in between
        and the heights to the exalted.

11. When the just ascend its various levels
        to receive their inheritance,

---

[6]cf Prov. 30:4.

with justice He raises up each one
   to the degree that accords with his labors;
each is stopped at the level
   whereof he is worthy,
there being sufficient levels in Paradise
   for everyone:
the lowest parts for the repentant,
   the middle for the righteous,
the heights for those victorious,
   while the summit is reserved for God's Presence.*

12. Noah made the animals live
   in the lowest part of the Ark;
in the middle part
   he lodged the birds,
while Noah himself, like the Deity,
   resided on the upper deck.
On Mount Sinai it was the people
   who dwelt below,
the priests round about it,
   and Aaron halfway up,
while Moses was on its heights,
   and the Glorious One on the summit.

13. A symbol of the divisions
   in that Garden of Life
did Moses trace out in the Ark
   and on Mount Sinai too;
he depicted for us the types of Paradise
   with all its arrangements:
harmonious, fair and desirable
   in all things—
in its height, its beauty,
   its fragrance, and its different species.
Here is the harbor of all riches,
   whereby the Church is depicted.

HYMN III

At the summit of Paradise stands the Tree of Life, whose glory is so great that it cannot be approached; indeed, for Adam and Eve any approach to it was effectively hedged off by the Tree of Knowledge, lower down the mountain, whose fruit they had been forbidden to eat. The serpent, however, manages to persuade them to disobey the divine commandment and to eat the forbidden fruit. This act of disobedience opens Adam's eye both to the higher state of glory which God had destined for Eve and him if only they had kept the commandment, and to the shame that failure to keep it had brought upon them. The consequence of their action is a judgment which is in fact self-imposed.

Ephrem here follows a tradition known from a number of early Christian writers that Adam and Eve had been created in an intermediate state; whether or not they would be raised to a higher state God leaves to the outcome of the exercise of their free will. This is a theme developed at greater length in the Commentary on Genesis II:14-23.

The Tree of Knowledge can be understood as playing the same role as the sanctuary veil: only those authorized to do so many penetrate inside it; Adam, like king Uzziah (2 Chron. 26), presumptuously tried to enter—with disastrous results.

1. As for that part of the Garden, my beloved,
        which is situated so gloriously
    at the summit of that height
        where dwells the Glory,
    not even its symbol
        can be depicted in man's thought;
    for what mind
        has the sensitivity
    to gaze upon it,
        or the faculties to explore it,
    or the capacity to attain to that Garden
        whose riches are beyond comprehension.

RESPONSE: Praise to Your Justice that crowns the
                victorious.

2. Perhaps that blessed tree,
        the Tree of Life,
    is, by its rays,
        the sun of Paradise;
    its leaves glisten,
        and on them are impressed
    the spiritual graces
        of that Garden.
    In the breezes the other trees
        bow down as if in worship
    before that sovereign
        and leader of the trees.

3. In the very midst He planted
        the Tree of Knowledge,[1]
    endowing it with awe,
        hedging it in with dread,
    so that it might straightway serve
        as a boundary to the inner region of Paradise.
    Two things did Adam hear
        in that single decree:
    that they should not eat of it[2]
        and that, by shrinking from it,
    they should perceive that it was not lawful
        to penetrate further, beyond that Tree.[3]

4. The serpent could not
        enter Paradise,
    for neither animal
        nor bird

---

[1] Gen. 2:9.
[2] Gen. 2:17.
[3] Gen. 3:7.

was permitted to approach
   the outer region of Paradise,
and Adam had to go out
   to meet them;
so the serpent cunningly learned,
   through questioning Eve,
the character of Paradise,
   what it was and how it was ordered.

5. When the accursed one learned
      how the glory of that inner Tabernacle,
   as if in a sanctuary,
      was hidden from them,
   and that the Tree of Knowledge,
      clothed with an injunction,
   served as the veil
      for the sanctuary,
   he realized that its fruit
      was the key of justice
   that would open the eyes of the bold
      —and cause them great remorse.

6. Their eyes were open*—
      though at the same time they were still closed
   so as not to see the Glory
      or their own low estate,
   so as not to see the Glory
      of that inner Tabernacle,
   nor to see the nakedness
      of their own bodies.
   These two kinds of knowledge
      God hid in the Tree,
   placing it as a judge
      between the two parties.

7. But when Adam boldly ran
        and ate of its fruit
    this double knowledge
        straightway flew toward him,
    tore away and removed
        both veils from his eyes:
    he beheld the Glory of the Holy of Holies
        and trembled;
    he beheld, too, his own shame and blushed,
        groaning and lamenting
    because the twofold knowledge he had gained
        had proved for him a torment.

8. Whoever has eaten
        of that fruit
    either sees and is filled with delight,
        or he sees and groans out.
    The serpent incited them to eat in sin
        so that they might lament;
    having seen the blessed state,
        they could not taste of it—
    like that hero of old*
        whose torment was doubled
    because in his hunger he could not taste
        the delights which he beheld.

9. For God had not allowed him
        to see his naked state,
    so that, should he spurn the commandment,
        his ignominy might be shown him.
    Nor did He show him the Holy of Holies,
        in order that, if he kept the command,
    he might set eyes upon it
        and rejoice.
    These two things did God conceal,
        as the two recompenses,

so that Adam might receive, by means of his contest,
    a crown that befitted his actions.

10. God established the Tree as judge,
    so that if Adam should eat from it,
it might show him that rank
    which he had lost through his pride,
and show him, as well, that low estate
    he had acquired, to his torment.
Whereas, if he should overcome and conquer,
    it would robe him in glory
and reveal to him also
    the nature of shame,
so that he might acquire, in his good health,
    an understanding of sickness.

11. A man, indeed, who has acquired
    good health in himself,
and is aware in his mind
    of what sickness is,
has gained something beneficial
    and he knows something profitable;
but a man who lies
    in sickness,
and knows in his mind
    what is good health,
is vexed by his sickness
    and tormented in his mind.

12. Had Adam conquered,*
    he would have acquired
glory upon his limbs,
    and discernment of what suffering is,
so that he might be radiant in his limbs
    and grow in his discernment.
But the serpent reversed all this

and made him taste
abasement in reality,
  and glory in recollection only,
so that he might feel shame at what he had found
  and weep at what he had lost.

13. The Tree was to him
       like a gate;
     its fruit was the veil
       covering that hidden Tabernacle.
     Adam snatched the fruit,
       casting aside the commandment.
     When he beheld that Glory
       within,
     shining forth with its rays,
       he fled outside;
     he ran off and took refuge
       among the modest fig trees.

14. In the midst of Paradise God had planted
       the Tree of Knowledge
     to separate off, above and below,
       sanctuary from Holy of Holies.
     Adam made bold to touch,
       and was smitten like Uzziah:*4
     the king became leprous,
       Adam was stripped.
     Being struck like Uzziah,
       he hastened to leave:
     both kings* fled and hid,
       in shame of their bodies.

15. Even though all the trees
       of Paradise

---

4 2 Chron. 26:16.

are clothed each in its own glory,
    yet each veils itself at the Glory;
the Seraphs with their wings,
    the trees with their branches,
all cover their faces so as not to behold
    their Lord.
They all blushed at Adam
    who was suddenly found naked;
the serpent had stolen his garments,
    for which it was deprived of its feet.*

16. God did not permit
    Adam to enter
that innermost Tabernacle;
    this was withheld,
so that first he might prove pleasing
    in his service of that outer Tabernacle;
like a priest
    with fragrant incense,
Adam's keeping of the commandment
    was to be his censer;
then he might enter before the Hidden One
    into that hidden Tabernacle.

17. The symbol of Paradise
    was depicted by Moses
who made the two sanctuaries,
    the sanctuary and the Holy of Holies;
into the outer one
    entrance was permitted,
but into the inner,
    only once a year.[5]
So too with Paradise,
    God closed off the inner part,
but He opened up the outer,
    wherein Adam might graze.

[5]Lev. 16; Heb. 9:7.

HYMN IV

Before the Fall, the Tree of Knowledge, with the commandment not to eat of it, had served as a boundary between Adam
and God's glory; after the Fall, however, Adam is kept at a
much greater distance, being henceforth prevented from entering Paradise at all by the "inviolate boundary" of the
cherub's sharp sword (Genesis 3:24). Paradise now abhors
Adam just as the Jewish Law abhorred the ritually unclean
leper, keeping him outside the Israelite camp, but, just as the
Law made provision for the leper's re-entry into Israelite
society, so too Christ the High Priest provides for the restoration of Adam/humanity to Paradise.

1. The Just One saw how Adam had become audacious
       because He had been lenient,
   and He knew that he would overstep again
       if He continued thus;
   Adam had trampled down
       that gentle and pleasant boundary,
   so instead God made for him
       a boundary guarded by force.
   The mere words of the commandment
       had been the boundary to the Tree,
   but now the cherub and the sharp sword
       provided the fence to Paradise.[1]

RESPONSE: Deem me worthy that through Your grace
             we may enter Your Paradise.

2. Adam in all his filth
       sought to enter
   that Holy of Holies
       which loves only those who resemble it;

---

[1]Gen. 3:24.

and because he made bold to enter
    that inner tabernacle,
God did not allow him to enter
    the outer one either.
When that sea full of life
    saw a corpse in its midst,
it did not leave it there
    but cast it forth.

3. Moses depicted the type
    among the people of the Hebrews:
when a man becomes leprous
    within the encampment
he is driven from its midst
    and cast outside;
while if he sloughs off his leprosy
    and makes supplication,[2]
the priest purifies him
    with hyssop, blood and water,[3]
and he returns to his former abode
    and enters into his inheritance.

4. Adam had been most pure
    in that fair Garden,
but he became leprous and repulsive
    because the serpent had breathed on him.
The Garden cast him from its midst;
    all shining, it thrust him forth.
The High Priest,[4] the Exalted One,
    beheld him
cast out from Himself:
    He stooped down and came to him,

[2]Lev. 13:46.
[3]Lev. 14:1-9.
[4]cf Hebr. 9:11.

He cleansed him with hyssop,
    and led him back to Paradise.

5. Adam had been naked and fair,
        but his diligent wife
    labored and made for him
        a garment covered with stains.
    The Garden, seeing him thus vile,
        drove him forth.
    Through Mary Adam had
        another robe*
    which adorned the thief;[5]
        and when he became resplendent at Christ's
        promise,
    the Garden, looking on,
        embraced him in Adam's place.

6. Moses who doubted
        saw but did not enter
    the land of God's promise;[6]
        the Jordan served as a boundary.
    Adam went astray and left
        the Garden of Life;
    the cherub became a fence.
        Both boundaries were set
    by the hand of our Lord,
        but at the Resurrection they both entered:
    Moses, into that land,
        and Adam, into Paradise.

7. The tongue cannot relate
        the description of innermost Paradise,
    nor indeed does it suffice
        for the beauties of the outer part;

---

[5]Luke 23:43.
[6]Deut. 32:50-52, 34:4.

for even the simple adornments
    by the Garden's fence
cannot be related
    in an adequate way.
For the colors of Paradise are full of joy,
    its scents most wonderful,
its beauties most desirable,
    and its delicacies glorious.

8. Even though the treasure
    that adjoins the fence is lowly,
yet it surpasses all other treasures
    in the world entire;
and by as much as the slopes, too,
    are lowly in comparison
with that treasury
    of the summit on high,
so the blessed state by the fence
    is more glorious and exalted
than all that we experience as blessed,
    who live in the valley below.

9. Be not angry that my tongue
    has presumed to describe a theme
too great for it,
    and so, through its own inadequacy, has
    diminished that greatness.
As there is no mirror adequate
    to reflect its beauty,
nor paints
    which may portray it,
then may my attempt not be rejected,
    for I have labored to compose
in my description of Paradise
    a means whereby we may gain profit.

10. The mourner can find comfort therein,
       the child be educated thereby,
    the chaste become radiant through it,
       the needy find provision from it.
    And so let each one of them throw me
       his little coin,*
    and may they all make supplication for me
       in Eden,
    so that I may enter that place
       whereof I have spoken in so far as I am able;
    and so that the downcast may become desirous
       of the riches that it promises.

11. May my purpose not be judged
       by You, O Knower of all things;
    may my search not be held blameworthy
       by You, concealed from all;
    for I have not made bold to speak
       of Your generation, hidden from all;
    in silence
       I have bounded the Word.
    Yet because I have honored Your birth,
       allow me to dwell in Your Paradise.
    From all who love You
       be praise to Your hiddenness!

HYMN V

Although from one point of view the Biblical text may seem to be something static like a rock (Exodus 17:6), in fact this rock accompanies those who make use of it (1 Corinthians 10:4) and from it flow streams of vivifying water. St Ephrem goes on to describe his own experience of being transported to Paradise as he read the Paradise narrative of Genesis. A practical question then raises itself in his mind: is there going to

be enough space there for everyone at the final Resurrection?
The analogy of a legion of demons inhabiting a single body
(Mark 5:9), however, reminds him that the resurrected body
will be of a different order from the physical, and so there is
in fact no problem. As he is transported back into this world
(stanza 11), he reflects on how misguided are those who weep
to leave this world of sorrows when Paradise is so full of
beauty (compare Hymn XIII).

1. I considered the Word of the Creator,
      and likened it
   to the rock that marched
      with the people of Israel in the wilderness;[1]
   it was not from the reservoir
      of water contained within it
   that it poured forth for them
      glorious streams:
   there was no water in the rock,
      yet oceans sprang forth from it;
   just so did the Word
      fashion created things* out of nothing.

RESPONSE: Blessed is that person accounted worthy
            to inherit Your Paradise.

2. In his book Moses
      described the creation of the natural world,
   so that both Nature and Scripture
      might bear witness to the Creator:*[2]
   Nature, through man's use of it,
      Scripture, through his reading of it.
   These are the witnesses
      which reach everywhere,

[1] Cor. 10:4.
[2] cf John 8:17.

they are to be found at all times,
 present at every hour,
confuting the unbeliever
 who defames the Creator.

3. I read the opening of this book
 and was filled with joy,
for its verses and lines
 spread out their arms to welcome me;
the first rushed out and kissed me,
 and led me on to its companion;
and when I reached that verse
 wherein is written
the story of Paradise,
 it lifted me up and transported me
from the bosom of the book
 to the very bosom of Paradise.

4. The eye and the mind
 traveled over the lines
as over a bridge, and entered together
 the story of Paradise.
The eye as it read
 transported the mind;
in return the mind, too,
 gave the eye rest
from its reading,
 for when the book had been read
the eye had rest,
 but the mind was engaged.

5. Both the bridge and the gate
 of Paradise
did I find in this book.
 I crossed over and entered;

my eye indeed remained outside
    but my mind entered within.
I began to wander
    amid things not described.
This is a luminous height,
    clear, lofty and fair:
Scripture named it Eden,[3]
    the summit of all blessings.

6. There too did I see
        the bowers of the just
    dripping with unguents
        and fragrant with scents,
    garlanded with fruits,
        crowned with blossoms.
    In accord with a person's deeds
        such was his bower;
    thus one had few adornments,
        while another was resplendent in its beauty;
    one was but dim in its coloring,
        while another dazzled in its glory.

7. I enquired into this too,
        whether Paradise
    was sufficient in size
        for all the righteous to live there.
    I asked about what is not written in Scripture,
        but my instruction came from what is written
        there:
    "Consider the man
        in whom there dwelt
    a legion of all kinds of demons;[4]
        they were there although not apparent,

---

[3]Gen. 2:8.
[4]Mark 5:9; Luke 8:30.

for their army is of a stuff finer and more subtle
    than the soul itself.

8. That whole army
        dwelt in a single body.
    A hundred times finer
        and more subtle
    are the bodies of the righteous
        when they are risen, at the Resurrection:
    they resemble the mind
        which is able,
    if it so wills, to stretch out and expand,
        or, should it wish, to contract and shrink;
    if it shrinks, it is in some place,
        if it expands, it is in every place.

9. Listen further
        and learn
    how lamps with thousands of rays
        can exist in a single house,
    how ten thousand scents
        can exist in a single blossom;
    though they exist within a small space,
        they have ample room
    to disport themselves.
        So it is with Paradise:
    though it is full of spiritual beings,
        it is amply spacious for their disportment.

10. Again, thoughts,
        infinite in number, dwell
    even in the small space of the heart,*
        yet they have ample room;
    they neither constrict each other,
        nor are they constricted there.

How much more will Paradise
    the glorious
suffice for the spiritual beings
    that are so refined in substance
that even thoughts
    cannot touch them!"

11. I gave praise as far as I was able
    and was on the point of departing
when, from the midst of Paradise,
    there came a sudden thunderous sound,
and, like the blare of trumpets
    in some camp,
a voice crying "holy"
    thrice over.[5]
Thus I knew that the divinity
    received praise in Paradise;
I had supposed it was empty,*
    but I learn otherwise from the thunderous sound.

12. Paradise delighted me
    as much by its peacefulness as by its beauty:
in it there resides a beauty
    that has no spot;
in it exists a peacefulness
    that knows no fear.
How blessed is that person
    accounted worthy to receive it,
if not by right,
    yet at least by grace;
if not because of good works,
    yet at least through mercy.

13. I was in wonder as I crossed
    the borders of Paradise

---

[5]Isaiah 6:3.

at how well-being, as though a companion,
    turned round and remained behind.
And when I reached the shore of earth,
    the mother of thorns,[6]
I encountered all kinds
    of pain and suffering.
I learned how, compared to Paradise,
    our abode is but a dungeon;
yet the prisoners within it
    weep when they leave it!

14. I was amazed at how even infants
    weep as they leave the womb—
weeping because they come out
    from darkness into light
and from suffocation they issue forth
    into this world!
Likewise death, too,
    is for the world
a symbol of birth,
    and yet people weep because they are born
out of this world, the mother of suffering,
    into the Garden of splendors.*

15. Have pity on me,
    O Lord of Paradise,
and if it is not possible for me
    to enter Your Paradise,
grant that I may graze
    outside, by its enclosure;
within, let there be spread
    the table for the "diligent,"*
but may the fruits within its enclosure
    drop outside like the "crumbs"[7]

---

[6]Gen. 3:18.
[7]Matt. 15:27 and parallels.

for sinners, so that, through Your grace,
    they may live!

HYMN VI

It is only when studied within the context of Orthodox
belief ("the keys of doctrine," stanza 1) that the Scriptures
become truly meaningful, allowing the reader/hearer of the
Paradise narrative to experience something of what Paradise
is really like. In stanzas 4-5 St Ephrem describes just such an
experience of the Garden's delights, and this simply serves to
deepen his awe and wonder at the original state of Adam and
Eve, for whose sake Paradise had been created. The Church
now corresponds to Paradise, and this correspondence can be
understood from two different aspects. On the one hand, we
are ourselves undergoing the same period of testing that Adam
and Eve underwent: whereas they were required to be obedient
to the commandment not to eat of the Tree, we are now
required to be obedient to Christ, whose fruit we are actually
permitted to eat daily (stanza 8); once again all depends on
our interior disposition and the proper exercise of the gift of
free will. On the other hand, those who have successfully exer-
cised this free will and have listened to Christ already experience the eschatological Paradise, and indeed themselves con-
stitute fruits even more glorious than those of Paradise's own
trees. This being so, the saints still on earth can be seen as
revealing Paradise to the rest of humanity. This state of affairs
indeed applied already under the Old Covenant, and it is from
this that St Ephrem enumerates a series of examples with which
the poem concludes.

1. The keys of doctrine
        which unlock all of Scripture's books,
    have opened up before my eyes
        the book of creation,

the treasure house of the Ark,
the crown of the Law.
This is a book which, above its companions,
has in its narrative
made the Creator perceptible
and transmitted His actions;
it has envisioned all His craftsmanship,
made manifest His works of art.

RESPONSE: Blessed is He who through His Cross
has flung open Paradise.

2. Scripture brought me
to the gate of Paradise,
and the mind, which is spiritual,
stood in amazement and wonder as it entered,
the intellect grew dizzy and weak
as the senses were no longer able
to contain its treasures—
so magnificent they were—
or to discern its savors
and find any comparison for its colors,
or take in its beauties
so as to describe them in words.

3. Paradise surrounds the limbs
with its many delights:
the eyes, with its handiwork,
the hearing, with its sounds,
the mouth and the nostrils,
with its tastes and scents.
Blessed is that person who has gathered for himself
the company of all
who have kept vigil and fasted;
they, in return for their fasts,

shall delight to graze
   upon its luxurious pastures.

4. Paradise raised me up as I perceived it,
      it enriched me as I meditated upon it;
   I forgot my poor estate,
      for it had made me drunk with its fragrance.
   I became as though no longer my old self,
      for it renewed me with all its varied nature.
   I swam around
      in its magnificent waves;
   and in the place that, burning like a furnace,
      had made Adam naked,
   I became so inebriated
      that I forgot all my sins there.

5. Although I was not sufficient
      for all the waves of its beauty,
   Paradise took me up and cast me
      into a sea still greater;
   in its fair beauty I beheld
      those who are far more beautiful than it,
   and I reflected:
      if Paradise be so glorious,
   how much more glorious should Adam be,
      who is in the image[1] of its Planter,
   and how much fairer the Cross,
      upon which the Son of its Lord rode.*

6. It was not Paradise
      that gave rise to the creation of mankind;
   rather, it was for Adam alone
      that Paradise had been planted,
   for to its buds Adam's heart is superior,
      to its fruits his words,

[1]Gen. 1:27.

because rational speech has more savor
   than the produce of Paradise;
truth in mankind
   surpasses its plants,*
and love is likewise more comely
   than its sweet scents.

7. God planted the fair Garden,
   He built the pure Church;[2]
upon the Tree of Knowledge
   He established the injunction.
He gave joy, but they took no delight,
   He gave admonition, but they were unafraid.
In the Church He implanted
   the Word
which causes rejoicing with its promises,
   which causes fear with its warnings:
he who despises the Word, perishes,
   he who takes warning, lives.

8. The assembly of saints
   bears resemblance to Paradise:
in it each day is plucked
   the fruit* of Him who gives life to all;
in it, my brethren, is trodden
   the cluster of grapes, to be the Medicine of Life.
The serpent is crippled and bound
   by the curse,[3]
while Eve's mouth is sealed
   with a silence that is beneficial[4]
—but it also serves once again
   as a harp to sing the praises of her Creator.

---

[2]Eph. 5:27.
[3]Gen. 3:14.
[4]1 Cor. 14:34.

9. Among the saints none is naked,
      for they have put on glory,
   nor is any clad in those leaves
      or standing in shame,
   for they have found, through our Lord,
      the robe that belongs to Adam and Eve.
   As the Church
      purges her ears
   of the serpent's poison,
      those who had lost their garments,
   having listened to it and become diseased,
      have now been renewed and whitened.*

10. The effortless power,
       the arm which never tires,
    planted this Paradise,
       adorned it without effort.
    But it is the effort of free will
       that adorns the Church with all manner of fruits.
    The Creator saw the Church
       and was pleased;
    He resided in that Paradise
       which she had planted for His honor,
    just as He had planted the Garden
       for her delight.

11. The diligent carry their own fruits
       and now run forward
    to meet Paradise
       as it exults with every sort of fruit.
    They enter that Garden
       with glorious deeds,
    and it sees
       that the fruits of the just
    surpass in their excellence
       the fruits of its own trees,

and that the adornments of the victorious
   outrival its own.

12. Happy indeed is the person accounted worthy
      to behold in Paradise
   the glorious fruits of the trees
      which so surpass—
   but which then take second place
      once they behold the fruits of the victorious!
   The flowers of Paradise took the victory,
      but then were vanquised
   at the sight of the blossoms
      of the celibate and chaste*
   at whose garlands
      both creation and its Creator rejoice.

13. The fruits of the righteous
      were more pleasing to the Knower of all
   than the fruits
      and produce of the trees.
   The beauty that exists in nature
      extolled the human mind,
   and Paradise lauded
      the intellect;
   the flowers gave praise to virtuous life,
      the Garden to free will,
   and the earth to human thought.
      Blessed is He who made Adam so great!

14. More fitting to be told
      than the glorious account
   of Paradise
      are the exploits of the victorious
   who adorned themselves
      with the very likeness of Paradise;

in them is depicted
　　the beauty of the Garden.
Let us take leave of the trees
　　and tell of the victors,
instead of the inheritance
　　let us celebrate the inheritors.

15. If the beauty of Paradise
　　　strikes us with astonishment,
　　how much more should we be astonished
　　　at beauty of the mind:
　　one is the product of nature,
　　　the other of the will.
　　Free will was envious
　　　of the Garden
　　and from itself brought forth
　　　victorious fruits
　　whose crowns vanquish
　　　the very spendors of Paradise.

16. There, manifest and fair
　　　to the eye of the mind,
　　are the coveted banquets of the just
　　　who summon us
　　to be their companions and brothers,
　　　their fellow members.
　　Let us not be deprived, my brethren,
　　　of their company;
　　let us be their kindred,
　　　or failing that, their neighbors,
　　and if not in their own dwelling,
　　　at least round about their bowers.

17. How enviable is that person
　　　held worthy of their treasuries' wealth,

how blessed is that person
   held worthy of even the dregs of their riches.
O make me worthy of that least part
   which comes from there;
may the enemy see me
   and be stricken with gloom,
for he imagined he would see me
   in the place he had made ready for me;
may he now behold me in that place
   which Your mercy has prepared for me!

18. Blessed is the person who is worthy
     to look upon their raiment,
  blessed is the person who is worthy
    and has heard their wisdom,
  blessed are the ears
    that have drunk to the full of their voices,
  blessed is the person who has achieved
    their blessed state,
  blessed the person who has toiled
    to be among the first,
  woe to him who made no effort
    even to be among the last.[5]

19. Blessed indeed is that person on whose behalf
     they have interceded before the Good One,
  woe to him whom they have opposed
    before the Just One.
  Those whom the Good One loves shall be in Eden,
    those whom the Just rejects, in Sheol.*
  The city against which they have shaken off
    the dust from their shoes
  will be in worse plight than Sodom;[6]
    but in the house where they have prayed

---

[5]Matt. 20:8 and parallels.
[6]Matt. 10:14-15 and parallels.

the dead will come to life[7]
and peace will reside throughout.

20. They went down to Egypt
and provided food when famine reigned;[8]
they came to the obstinate sea,
and taught it wisdom with a rod;[9]
they went out into the hostile desert
and adorned it with the pillar;[10]
they entered the furnace,
fiercely heated,[11]
and sprinkled it with their dew;[12]
into the pit where they had been thrown
an angel entered
and taught its wild beasts to fast.[13]

21. The Salt that seasoned itself
to prevent losing its savor[14]
had been scattered all over the world
by the hand of the Creator.
Just as His hand took from every quarter*
and created Adam,
so has he now been scattered
in every quarter.
The hand now gathers what had been scattered,
and scatters what had been gathered,
for progression is from the universe to Adam,
and then from him to the universe.

---

[7]cf Acts 20:9-12.
[8]Gen. 41:54-57.
[9]Exod. 14:16.
[10]Exod. 14:19.
[11]Dan. 3:19-28.
[12]Dan. 3:50.
[13]Dan. 6:22.
[14]Matt. 5:13 and parallels.

22. The East has grown luminous with the saints,
     with them the West has become brilliant,
   the North is raised up by them,
     from them the South has learned.
   They have ascended to the firmament and opened it,[15]
     they have gone down to the sea and explored it;[16]
   the mystery that the apostle revealed
     in a parable
   have they extended to all humankind,
     reaching every corner;[17]
   all creation has embraced it
     to draw strength from it.

23. One of them cleft
     the air with his chariot;[18]
   the Watchers rejoiced as they met him,
     seeing that a body
   had lately taken up its abode among them;
     and just as an earthly being
   ascended in a chariot
     and put on splendor,
   so did the Lord, in His grace,
     descend and put on a body;
   He then mounted a cloud and ascended[19]
     to reign over high and low.

24. The Watchers* of fire and spirit
     stood in wonder at Elias,
   seeing hidden within him
     the sweet treasure;

---

[15]cf 2 Cor. 12:3.
[16]cf 2 Cor. 11:25.
[17]cf Rom. 16:25-26, Col. 1:25-26.
[18]Elias (Elijah): 2 Kings 2:11.
[19]Acts 1:9.

in wonder at one formed of earth,
    they gave thanks to his Fashioner.
Seeing his virginity
    they exulted,
for it had exalted those below
    and caused wonder to those above,
its contest being on earth,
    its crown in Paradise.

25. With love and instruction,
        commingled with truth,
    the intellect can grow
        and become rich with new things,
    as it meditates with discernment
        on the treasure store of hidden mysteries.
    For my part, I have loved, and so learned,
        and become assured
    that Paradise possesses
        the haven of the victorious.
    As I have been held worthy to perceive it,
        so make me worthy to enter it!

HYMN VII

Whereas Adam and Eve had just God's commandment, we also have His promise; let this serve as a source of comfort in times of temptation. The examples of the saints, whose fruits are even fairer than those of Paradise, are there too to encourage us; so varied are the lives of the saints that everyone will find some special example among them to rejoice in and to follow. St Ephrem concludes on a characteristic personal note: contemplation of the saints also serves to rebuke him for his own sins and to make him reflect how, in seeking to please our fellow human beings rather than God, we have all too often exchanged freedom for slavery.

1. In times of temptation
        console yourselves with God's promises,
    for there is no deceit
        in the word of Him who repays all,
    and His treasure house is not so paltry
        that we should doubt His promise;
    He has surrendered His own Son for us
        so that we might believe in Him;
    His Body is with us,
        His assurance is with us,
    He came and gave us His keys,
        since it is for us that His treasures lie waiting.

RESPONSE: Blessed is He who, with His keys,
                has opened up the Garden of Life.

2. In the evening the world sleeps,
        closing its eyes,
    while in the morning it arises.
        He who repays is distant
    as it were but a night's length away;
        now light dawns and He is coming.
    Weary not, my brethren,
        nor suppose
    that your struggle will last long,
        or that your resurrection is far off,
    for our death is already behind us,
        and our resurrection before us.

3. Bear up, O life of mourning,*
        so that you may attain to Paradise;
    its dew will wash off your squalor,
        while what it exudes will render you fragrant;
    its support will afford rest after your toil,
        its crown will give you comfort,

it will proffer you fruits
   in your hunger,
fruits that purify those who partake of them;
   in your thirst
it will provide for you a celestial draught,
   one that makes wise those who drink of it.

4. Blessed is the poor man
     who gazes on that place;
   riches are poured in profusion
     outside and around it;
   chalcedony and other gems[1]
     lie there cast out
   to prevent their defiling
     the glorious earth of Paradise;
   should someone place there
     precious stones or beryls,
   these would appear ugly and dull
     compared with that dazzling land.

5. Both men and women
     are clothed in raiment of light;
   the garments provided to cover their nakedness
     are swallowed up in glory;
   all the limbs' vile emotions
     are silenced,
   the fountains of lust
     are stopped up,
   anger is removed
     and the soul purified
   and, like wheat, it flourishes in Eden,
     unchoked by thorns.

6. There virginity dances
     because the serpent,

---

[1] cf Ezek. 28:13.

who secretly poured venom into her ears,
  is now destroyed;
the fig rushes up to her
  and full of joy exclaims:
"Put away your ignorant
  childhood—
the day when you became naked
  and hid in my bosom.
Praise to Him who has clothed
  your nakedness with the robe!"

7. There youth exults
  because of what it has achieved;
in Paradise it beholds
  Joseph who stripped off*
and cast away the lust
  that flared up among the senseless;[2]
it sees too the child who overcame the asp
  in its hole.[3]
Samson overcame a lion,
  but a viper conquered
and smote him, causing him straightway to lose
  his Nazirite locks.[4]

8. There the married state
  finds rest after having been anguished
by the pangs of giving birth, brought on by the curse,[5]
  and by the pain of childbearing;
now it sees the children
  whom it had buried amid laments,
pasturing like lambs
  in Eden;

[2]Gen. 39:10.
[3]Isaiah 11:8.
[4]Judges 14:6, 16:16-19.
[5]Gen. 3:16.

exalted in their ranks,
   glorious in their splendors,
they are like kindred
   of the spotless angels.

9. Thanks be to the Merciful One
       who plucked them while still young—
    the children who are
       the late fruits
    to become in Paradise
       the first fruits* of all.
    A novel sight may be seen there:
       these "fruits" pluck
     the fruiting produce,
       the firstlings pluck the firstfruits.
    In their purity both plucked
       and plucker are alike.

10. Bind up your thoughts, Old Age,
       in Paradise
    whose fragrance makes you young;
       its wafting scent rejuvenates you,
    and your stains are swallowed up
       in the beauty with which it clothes you.
    In Moses He depicted for you
       a parable:
    his cheeks, ashen with age,
       became shining and fair,[6]
    a symbol of old age
       that in Eden again becomes young.

11. No blemish is in them,
       for they are without wickedness;

---

[6]Exod. 34:29.

no anger is in them,
  for they have no fiery temper;
no mocking scorn is in them,
  for they are without guile.
They do not race to do harm—
  and so themselves be harmed;
they show no hatred there,
  for there they are without envy;
they pronounce no judgment there,
  for there no oppression exists.

12. People behold themselves
      in glory
  and wonder at themselves,
      discovering where they are.
  The nature of their bodies,
      once troubled and troublesome,
  is now tranquil and quiet,
      resplendent
  from without in beauty,
      and from within with purity,
  the body in evident ways,
      the soul in hidden ways.

13. In Paradise the cripples,
      who had never walked, leap around;
  the deformed, who had never even crawled,
      fly about through the air;
  the eyes of the blind and deaf,
      who had yearned from the womb,
  hungering for the light
      which they had failed to see,
  now rejoice to behold
      the beauty of Paradise,
  and the mighty sound of its harps
      gives comfort to their ears.

14. At him who has uttered
    no curse or abuse
does Paradise's blessing
    rejoice all the more;
upon him whose eyes' glance
    remained always chaste
does Paradise's beauty
    gaze the more;
in the limbs of him
    who quelled the venom of his thoughts
do its springs of sweetness
    well up.

15. The virgin who rejected
    the marriage crown that fades
now has the radiant marriage chamber
    that cherishes the children of light,
shining out because she rejected
    the works of darkness.
To her who was alone
    in a lonely house
the wedding feast now grants tranquility:
    here angels rejoice,
prophets delight,
    and apostles add splendor.

16. Fasters, who have chosen Daniel's
    meager diet of vegetables[7]
  —and before Daniel kings with their crowns
    bowed down and did reverence—
fasters like these do the trees,
    not kings, extol,
bowing down in all their beauty
    and inviting them

---

[7]Dan. 1:12.

    to turn aside to the place where they grow,
        and take up their abode amid their boughs,
    bathe in their dew
        and rejoice in their fruits.

17. Whoever has washed the feet of the saints
        will himself be cleansed in that dew;
    to the hand that has stretched out
        to give to the poor
    will the fruits of the trees
        themselves stretch out;
    the very footsteps of him
        who visited the sick in their affliction
    do the flowers make haste
        to crown with blooms,
    jostling to see
        which can be first to kiss his steps.

18. The man who abstained,
        with understanding, from wine,
    will the vines of Paradise
        rush out to meet, all the more joyfully,
    as each one stretches out and proffers him
        its clusters;
    or if any has lived
        a life of virginity,
    him too they welcome into their bosom,
        for the solitary such as he
    has never lain in any bosom
        nor upon any marriage bed.*

19. Those who have been crowned for our Lord's sake
        with the martyr's death by the sword
    shine out in glory there
        with their crowns

because their bodies despised
   the persecutors' fire.
Like stars[8] do they blossom
   in Paradise,
those seven sons of light*
   with their radiant mother,
who, in their deaths,
   spurned the wrath of the impious king.[9]

20. The happiness of this place
     gives joy to the women who labored
  in the service of the saints:
     there they see that widow
  who took in Elias[10]
     savor Eden's delights;
  instead of those two fountains
     —the jar and the cruse—
  which gave her her livelihood,
     now the boughs of the trees
  provide this in Eden
     for all women who have given livelihood to the
     poor.

21. Nothing there in Paradise
     is useless*:
  both grass and roots
     bring benefit and profit;
  whoever tastes them is rejuvenated,
     whoever breathes in their scent grows fair;
  in the bosom of its blossoms and flowers
     is hidden

---

[8]Dan. 12:3.
[9]2 Macc. 7.
[10]1 Kings 17:14.

a veritable treasure,
a gift for those who pluck it;
the fruits of Paradise bear rich wealth
for those who gather them.

22. None toil there,
for none go hungry there;
none endure shame there,
for none do wrong there;
none feel contrition there,
for there is no cause to repent there.
Those who run the course
find rest and quiet.
None grow old there,
for none die there;
none are buried there,
for none are born there.

23. They know no worry,
for they have no suffering;
they have no fear,
for no snare awaits them;
they have no adversary,
for they have passed through the contest.
They count themselves
blessed
unendingly,
for their warfare is over;
they have taken up their crowns
and found rest in their new abode.

24. I saw that place, my brethren,
and I sat down and wept,
for myself and for those like me,
at how my days have reached their fill,

dissipated one by one, faded out,[11]
    stolen away without my noticing;
remorse seizes hold of me
    because I have lost
crown, name* and glory,
    robe and bridal chamber of light.
How blessed is the person
    who of that heavenly table is held worthy!

25. May all the children of light
    make supplication for me there,
that our Lord may grant them
    the gift of a single soul.
Thus would I have renewed occasion
    to praise Him
whose hand is, to be sure,
    stretched out in readiness.
May He who gives
    both in justice and in grace
give to me, in His mercy,
    of the treasure store of His mercies.

26. And if none who is defiled
    can enter that place,
then allow me to live by its enclosure,
    residing in its shade.
Since Paradise resembles
    that table,
let me, through Your grace,
    eat of the "crumbs" of its fruit
which fall outside,
    so that I too may join
those dogs who had their fill
    from the crumbs of their masters' tables.[12]

---

[11] cf Ps. 89(90):9
[12] Matt. 15:27 and parallels.

27. And may I learn how much I will then have received
       from that parable of the Rich Man[13]
    who did not even give to the poor man
       the leftovers from his banquet;
    and may I see Lazarus,
       grazing in Paradise,
    and look upon the Rich Man,
       in anguish,
    so that the might of justice outside
       may cause me fear,
    but the breath of grace within
       may bring me comfort.

28. Allow me to dwell by the enclosure
       of that Garden, so that I may be
    a neighbor to those within,
       envied by those outside.
    Yet who is able to look, at the same time,
       on delight and torment,
    to behold both Gehenna
       and the Garden?
    May the crown of those within
       rebuke me for all my sins;
    may the punishment of those without
       teach me how great is Your mercy toward me.

29. Who can endure
       to look on both sides,
    whose ears can stand
       the terrible cries of the wicked,
    who proclaim, in Gehenna,
       that the Just One is righteous,
    while the good utter praise
       in the Garden?

---

[13]Luke 16:19.

The two sides gaze on each other
   in amazement,
the works of each side, revealed,
   serve to admonish the other.

30.   May my sins not be revealed
     to my brethren on that day,
   —yet by this we show
     how contemptible we are, Lord;
   if our sins are revealed to You,
     from whom can we hide them?
   I have made shame
     an idol for myself;
   grant me, Lord, to fear You,
     for You are mighty.
   May I feel shame and self-reproach
     before You, for You are gentle.

31.   A man's neighbor has become his god:
     every moment he seeks to please him;
   if he does wrong, he feels shame before him,
     if he does him an injury, he is afraid;
   or if he does him some good,
     then he has spoiled that good by his thirst for
     praise.
   Such a man has become an abject slave
     in all these ways.
   The Good One gave us freedom,
     but we have reduced this to slavery.
   May we exchange, for Your lordship,
     this overlord we have made for ourselves!

HYMN VIII

St Ephrem takes comfort from the last minute repentance of the Good Thief, but this leads him on to a quandary concerning the relationship of the soul to the body in Paradise. Although he finds himself unable to offer any way out of the problems raised by Christ's words, "this day you will be with me in Paradise" (Luke 23:43), St Ephrem is quite clear in his mind that the soul cannot enter Paradise without the body, and so the righteous cannot in fact enter Paradise until the final Resurrection, when the body and soul will eventually be reunited; in the meantime the disembodied souls await the Resurrection just outside the boundary of Paradise in a state that other Syriac writers describe as "the sleep of the soul."

1. There came to my ear
       from the Scripture which had been read
    a word that caused me joy
       on the subject of the Thief;[1]
    it gave comfort to my soul
       amidst the multitude of its vices,
    telling how He had compassion on the Thief.
       O may He bring me too
    into that Garden at the sound of whose name
       I am overwhelmed by joy;
    my mind bursts its reins
       as it goes forth to contemplate Him.

RESPONSE: Hold me worthy that we may become
              heirs in Your kingdom.

2. I behold a dwelling there
       and a tabernacle of light,

---

[1]Luke 23:39-43.

a voice proclaiming
   "Blessed is the Thief
who has freely received
   the keys to Paradise."
I imagined that he was already there,
   but then I considered
how the soul cannot
   have perception of Paradise
without its mate, the body,
   its instrument and lyre.

3. In this place of joys
   anguish seized me
as I realized that it is not profitable
   to delve into hidden things.
With respect to the Thief
   a dilemma beset me:
if the soul were able
   to see and to hear
without its body,
   why then is it confined therein?
And if the body is no longer alive,
   why should the soul be put to death with it?

4. That the soul cannot see
   without the body's frame,
the body itself persuades,
   since if the body becomes blind
the soul is blind in it,
   groping about with it;
see how each looks
   and attests to the other,
how the body has need of the soul
   in order to live,
and the soul too requires the body
   in order to see and to hear.

5. If the body grows deaf,
        the soul does too,
    and it grows delirious
        when the body reels with sickness.
    Though the soul exists
        of itself and for itself,
    yet without its companion
        it lacks true existence;
    it fully resembles an embryo
        still in the womb,
    whose existence is as yet
        bereft of word or thought.

6. If the soul, while in the body,
        resembles an embryo
    and is unable to know
        either itself or its companion,
    how much more feeble will it then be
        once it has left the body,
    no longer possessing on its own
        the senses
    which are able to serve
        as tools for it to use.
    For it is through the senses of its companion
        that it shines forth and becomes evident.

7. That blessed abode
        is in no way deficient,
    for that place is complete and perfected
        in every way,
    and the soul cannot
        enter there alone,
    for in such a state it is in everything
        deficient—
    in sensation and consciousness;
        but on the day of Resurrection

the body, with all its senses,
   will enter in as well, once it has been made perfect.

8. When the hand of the Creator
      fashioned and formed the body
   so that it might sing hymns
      to its Maker,
   this lyre was silent
      and had not voice,
   until at last
      He breathed into it
   the soul which sang therein.
      Thus the strings acquired sound,
   and the soul, by means of the body,
      acquired speech to utter wisdom.

9. When Adam
      was in all things complete,
   then the Lord took him
      and placed him in Paradise.
   The soul could not enter there
      of itself and for itself,
   but together they entered,
      body and soul,
   pure and perfect to that perfect place—
      and together they left it, once they had become
      sullied.
   From all this we should learn
      that at the Resurrection they will enter again
      together.

10. Adam was heedless
       as guardian of Paradise,
    for the crafty thief
       stealthily entered;

leaving aside the fruit
  —which most men would covet—
he stole instead
  the Garden's inhabitant!
Adam's Lord came out to seek him;
  He entered Sheol and found him there,
then led and brought him out
  to set him once more in Paradise.

11. Thus in the delightful mansions
      on the borders of Paradise
    do the souls of the just
      and righteous reside,
    awaiting there
      the bodies they love,
    so that, at the opening
      of the Garden's gate,
    both bodies and souls might proclaim,
      amidst Hosannas,
    "Blessed is He who has brought Adam from Sheol
      and returned him to Paradise in the company of
      many."[2]

HYMN IX

St Ephrem now turns to the joys of Paradise which the righteous will experience at the Resurrection; these can only be described by means of both analogy and contrast with life on earth. Just as air is essential for all life here, so too in Paradise is it the spiritual counterpart of air which sustains all transfigured existence there (throughout this hymn one should recall that in Syriac the term *ruha* means both "wind" and "spirit/Spirit"). In order to appreciate the spiritual beauty

[2]cf Matt. 27:52.

of Paradise we need to refine and purify our vision; provided
we do this, God will meet our desire for Him in whatever way
is most appropriate for each individual.

1. In the world there is struggle,
        in Eden, a crown of glory.
    at our resurrection
        both earth and heaven will God renew,[1]
    liberating all creatures,
        granting them paschal joy, along with us.
    Upon our mother Earth, along with us,[2]
        did He lay disgrace
    when He placed on her, with the sinner, the curse;
        so, together with the just, will He bless her too;
    this nursing mother, along with her children,
        shall He who is Good renew.

RESPONSE: Blessed is He who, in His Paradise,
                    gives joy to our gloom.

2. The evil one mixed his cup,
        proffering its bitterness to all;
    in everyone's path has he set his snares,
        for everyone has he spread out his net;
    he has caused tares to spring up
        in order to choke the good seed.[3]
    But in His glorious Paradise
        He who is Good
    will sweeten their bitter trials,
        their crowns He will make great;

---

[1] Isaiah 65:17, 66:22.
[2] cf Rom. 8:21.
[3] Matt. 13:25 and parallels.

because they have borne their crosses[4]
He will escort them into Eden.

3. Should you wish
   to climb up a tree,
   with its lower branches
   it will provide steps before your feet,
   eager to make you recline
   in its bosom above,
   on the couch of its upper branches.
   So arranged is the surface of these branches,
   bent low and cupped
   —while yet dense with flowers—
   that they serve as a protective womb
   for whoever rests there.

4. Who has ever beheld such a banquet
   in the very bosom of a tree,
   with fruit of every savor
   ranged for the hand to pluck.
   Each type of fruit in due sequence approaches,
   each awaiting its turn:
   fruit to eat,
   and fruit to quench the thirst;
   to rinse the hands there is dew,
   and leaves to dry them with after
   —a treasure store which lacks nothing,
   whose Lord is rich in all things.

5. Around the trees the air is limpid
   as the saints recline;
   below them are blossoms,
   above them fruit;
   fruits serve as their sky,
   flowers as their earth.

---

[4]Matt. 10:38 and parallels.

Who has ever heard of
   or seen
a cloud of fruits providing shade
   for the head,
or a garment of flowers
   spread out beneath the feet?

6. Such is the flowing brook of delights
     that, as one tree takes leave of you,
  the next one beckons to you;
     all of them rejoice
  that you should partake of the fruit of one
    and suck the juice of another,
  wash and cleanse yourself
    in the dew of yet a third;
  anoint yourself with the resin of one
    and breathe another's fragrance,
  listen to the song of still another.
    Blessed is He who gave joy to Adam!

7. Scented breezes blow
    with varied force;
  like Martha and Mary,
    they hasten with delicate foods,
  for the guests at this banquet
    never have to depart at all.
  Weary Martha[5]
    made so bold
  as to complain to Him
    who invites us to His Paradise
  where those who minister
    never weary in their service.

---

[5]Luke 10:40.

8. The breezes of Paradise
     hasten to attend to the just:
   one blows satiety,
     another quenches the thirst;
   this one is laden with goodness,
     that one with all that is rich.
   Who has ever beheld breezes
     acting as waiters,
   some offering foods,
     others diverse drinks,
   one breathing dew,
     another fragrant scents?

9. In a spiritual way do these breezes
     suckle spiritual beings:
   this is a feast where no hand labors
     or ever grows tired;
   the teeth do not weary,
     the stomach never grows heavy.
   Who has ever reclined and enjoyed himself
     without anyone slaving away?
   Who has eaten to satisfaction without any food,
     or drunk and become merry without any drink?

10. In seedlings you can observe
      symbols clearly marked.
    When the wind gives suck
      to wheat and to the ears of corn,
    it nourishes them as it blows,
      by its force it fattens them up.
    How much more should those winds
      full of blessing
    give suck to the seedlings of Paradise
      which are both rational and spiritual?
    For that which is spiritual
      has the Spirit's breath as its nourishment.

11. Breezes full of discernment
         nourish the discerning;
     this breeze provides you with nourishment in
     abundance,
         that one delights you as it blows,
     one causes your countenance to shine,
         while another gives you enjoyment.
     Who has ever experienced
         delight in this way,
     eating, without employing his hands,
         drinking, without using his mouth?
     As both cupbearer and baker
         do these delightful breezes act.

12. Even today on this earth of thorns[6]
         we can see in the field
     the spikes of wheat which God,
         despite those curses, has given:
     cradled within them, the grains receive their birth,
         thanks to the wind;
     at the good will of the Most High,
         who can perform all things,
     does the breeze suckle them,
         like a mother's breast it nurtures them,
     so that herein may be depicted a type
         of how spiritual beings are nourished.

13. If the grain of wheat
         which gives sustenance to our bodies
     (though most of it, as refuse,
         the body evacuates)
     —if the grain is nourished by the air,
         fattened by the wind,

---

[6]Gen. 3:18.

      how much more, in their refinement,
        can the breezes
      from Eden's treasure store
        bestow on spiritual beings
      etherial juices
        and foods that are spiritual.

14. Learn too from the fire
      how the air's breath is all-nourishing;
    if fire is confined
      in a place without air,
    its flame starts to flicker
      as it gasps for breath.
    Who has ever beheld
      a mother give suck
    with her whole being to everything?
      Upon her hangs the whole universe,
    while she depends on the One
      who is that Power which nourishes all.

15. The Chaldeans* are thus put to shame:
      for they exalted the stars,
    saying that it is they alone
      which give to the world all its nourishment.
    But it is the air which gives suck
      unstintingly
    to the stars as well as to seedlings,
      to reptiles and to man.
    This we are taught by the fire
      which itself is nourished by air,
    —and fire has a close affinity
      with those heavenly luminaries.

16. For if the soul
      flies away when air is absent—

since air is the body's pillar
    upon which our frame is supported,
being the bread of our bread,
    on which our own "field" grows fat—
how much the more, then,
    can this blessed air
give to spiritual beings pleasure
    as they partake and drink of it,
fly about and swim in it—
    this veritable ocean of delights?

17. Instead of bread, it is the very fragrance of Paradise
        that gives nourishment;
    instead of liquid,
        this life-giving breeze does service:
    the senses delight
        in its luxuriant waves
    which surge up
        in endless variety,
    with joyous intensity.
        Being unburdened,
    the senses stand in awe and delight
        before the divine Majesty.

18. Today our bodies grow hungry
        and have to be fed,
    but yonder it is souls,
        instead of bodies, that crave food.
    The soul receives sustenance
        appropriate to its needs;
    it is by the Nourisher of all
        that the soul receives its fill,
    and not by any other
        variety of food;
    it pastures on His beauties,
        full of wonder at His treasures.

19. Bodies,
>   with their flow of blood,
>   receive refinement there
>>   after the manner of souls;
>   the soul that is heavy
>>   has its wings refined
>   so that they resemble
>>   resplendent thought.
>   Thought, too, whose movements
>>   are ever in a state of disturbance,
>   will become unperturbed,
>>   after the pattern of that Majesty.

20. Far more glorious than the body
>   is the soul,
>   and more glorious still than the soul
>   is the spirit,
>   but more hidden than the spirit
>   is the Godhead.
>   At the end
>>   the body will put on
>   the beauty of the soul,
>>   the soul will put on that of the spirit,
>   while the spirit shall put on
>>   the very likeness of God's majesty.

21. For bodies shall be raised
>   to the level of souls,
>   and the soul
>   to that of the spirit,
>   while the spirit will be raised
>   to the height of God's majesty;
>   clinging to both awe
>>   and love,
>   it neither circles too high,
>>   nor holds back too much,

it discerns when to hold back,
   so that its flight is beneficial.

22. But if you are greedy
      Moses will reproach you;
   he took no provisions
      as he ascended to the mountain summit;[7]
   he was richly sustained because he hungered,
      he shone with much beauty because he thirsted.
   Who has ever beheld
      a famished man
   devour a vision and grow beautiful,
      imbibe a voice and be sustained?
   Nourished with the divine glory
      he grew and shone forth.

23. All that we eat
      the body eventually expels
   in a form that disgusts us;
      we are repelled by its smell.
   The burden of food debilitates us,
      in excess it proves harmful,
   but if it be joy
      which inebriates and sustains,
   how greatly will the soul be sustained
      on the waves of this joy
   as its faculties suck
      the breast of all wisdom.

24. Torrents of delight
      flow down through the First Born
   from the radiance of the Father
      upon the gathering of seers:

---

[7]Exod. 34.

they indulge themselves there
upon the pasture of divine visions.
Who has ever beheld the hungry
find satisfaction,
fare sumptuously and become inebriated
on waves of glory
flowing from the beauty
of that sublime Beauty?

25. The Lord of all
is the treasure store of all things:
upon each according to his capacity
He bestows a glimpse
of the beauty of His hiddenness,
of the splendor of His majesty.
He is the radiance who, in his love,
makes everyone shine
—the small, with flashes of light from Him,
the perfect, with rays more intense,
but only His Child is sufficient
for the might of His glory.

26. Accordingly as each here on earth
purifies his eye for Him,
so does he become more able to behold
His incomparable glory;
accordingly as each here on earth
opens his ear to Him,
so does he become more able to grasp
His wisdom;
accordingly as each here on earth
prepares a receptacle for Him,
so is he enabled to carry
a small portion of His riches.

27. The Lord who is beyond measure
    measures out nourishment to all,
adapting to our eyes the sight of Himself,
    to our hearing His voice,
His blessing to our appetite,
    His wisdom to our tongue.
At His gift
    blessings swarm,
for this is always new in its savor,
    wonderfully fragrant,
adaptable in its strength,
    resplendent in its colors.

28. Who has ever beheld gatherings of people
    whose sustenance is the giving of praise?
Their raiment is light,
    their countenance full of radiance;
as they ruminate
    on the abundance of His gift
there burst forth from their mouths
    springs of wisdom;
tranquility reigns over their thought,
    truth over their knowledge,
reverence over their enquiry,
    and love over their offering of praise.

29. Grant, Lord, that I and those dear to me
    may together there
find the very last remnants[8]
    of Your gift!
Just the sight of Your Dear One
    is a fountain of delight;
whoever is worthy
    to be ravished thereby

---

[8]Mark 8:8.

will despise ordinary food;
   all who look upon You
will be sustained by Your beauty.
   Praises be to Your splendor!

HYMN X

St Ephrem here contrasts the climate of Paradise, and its
cycle of seasons, with that of our earth. The earth's climate,
with its unruly storms during the bitterly cold winter months
and the torrid heat of the summer, shares in the fallen character
of humanity on earth, and so is incompatible with Paradise.
In Paradise, by contrast, the months follow a gentle and orderly
cycle of seasonal produce, and within each month the waxing
and waning of the moon governs the development of plant life,
a development which Ephrem compares to the human life cycle
(in order to emphasize his theme of rejuvenation, he lists the
course of the human cycle in reverse, starting with the aged
and ending up with the child as yet unborn).

For penitent sinners living on the slopes below, mere
proximity to Paradise has a healing effect. This thought however, makes Ephrem wonder whether he is not overbold in
positing such a place in the eschatological Paradise situated
"between the Garden and Hell's fire"; but in the final stanza
he takes comfort in the thought that, as God's divine cloud
hovers over the whole of creation, good and bad alike, so too
the dew of his overflowing compassion will reach even to
Gehenna in its effects.

1. What mouth
      has ever described Paradise,

what tongue
   has told of its glory,
what mind has depicted
   its beauty?
Indeed its hidden recesses
   cannot be scrutinized;
I can only marvel at what is visible,
   at those things which lie outside Paradise,
and so I realize how far I remain
   from its hidden secrets.

RESPONSE: Grant us to see Your righteous ones in
         Your Paradise.

2. In the temperate atmosphere
     that surrounds its outer boundary
  the months that pass by there
     are also temperate:
  there dismal February
     resembles radiant May,
  January with its
     icy blasts
  is like August with its fruits;
     June is like April
  and torrid July
     has September's dews.

3. Our feeble months take on Eden's delights*
     in the atmosphere
  that surrounds Eden,
     for Eden makes them like itself.
  The months blossom with flowers
     all around Paradise
  in order to weave
     throughout every season

a wreath of blossom
to embellish the slopes of Paradise,
being themselves not worthy
to provide a crown for the summit.

4. Because the months
are stricken by storms
they cannot enter Paradise,
so still in its tranquility.
If all the months' tempests
are overcome
in that atmosphere
outside Paradise,
how can they pollute
the glorious air
whose heavenly* breath
restores humanity to life?

5. The air of this earth
is wanton as a prostitute
with whom the twelve months
consort:
each one in turn
makes her comply with its own whims
while she produces fruits
from them all;
whereas the chaste* and pure air
of Paradise
is unpolluted in its purity
by the dalliance of the months.

6. There the abundant flow
of their produce is ceaseless,
for each month bears its own fruit,
its neighbor, flowers.

There the springs of delights
   open up and flow
with wine, milk, honey
   and cream.
Grass flourishes in December,
   after it January produces wheat;
February, divested of its cold and now radiant,
   bears sheaves in Paradise.

7. The months are divided
    into four groups:
the firstfruits show themselves
   in the first three months,
in the next three
   come the luscious soft fruits,
the seventh to ninth months
   ripen
the late fruits,
   while at the end, the year's crown,
the pregnant buds
   are bursting forth with joy.

8. The phases of the moon
    produce variation in the flowers;
at the beginning of the months
   the branches open up their buds*;
at full moon they blossom,
   ripening in every direction,
to subside once again
   at each month's completion.
They sink down as one month ends
   to sprout forth when the next begins;
the month furnishes the key
   for the opening and closing of their buds.

9. Who has ever beheld
       flowers with pregnant wombs
    which each month brings to pangs of labor,
       then, suddenly, to give birth?
    As the month increases,
       so do the flowers mirror its progress;
    at full moon they reach maturity,
       blossoming out,
    while as the month advances
       toward old age
    the flowers too grow old,
       only to be rejuvenated as the next is born.

10. Each month's fruits and flowers
       possess individually
    their own particular treasures,
       but when these are cross fertilized, they multiply:
    when two neighboring flowers,
       each with its distinctive color
    are crossed
       to become one,
    they produce a new color.
       When fruits are thus crossed
    they create a new and beautiful offspring
       whose foliage is different.

11. In Paradise the life cycle of the trees
       resembles a necklace:
    when the fruits of the first
       are finished and plucked,
    then the second ones are ready,
       with a third species following them.
    Who has ever beheld
       the autumnal fruits
    grasping the heels
       of the first fruits,

just as Jacob grasped hold
   of his brother's heel?[1]

12. That cornucopia full of fruits
     in all stages of development
  resembles the course
    of human marriage;
  it contains the old,
    young and middle-aged,
  children who have already been born,
    and babies still unborn;
  its fruits follow one another
    and appear
  like the continuous succession
    of humankind.

13. The river of humanity
    consists of people of all ages,
  with old, young,
    children and babes,
  infants in their mothers' arms
    and others still unborn, in the womb.
  Such is the sequence
    of Paradise's fruit:
  firstfruits issued forth
    with the autumn harvest,
  wave upon wave,
    fecund with blossoms and fruit.

14. Blessed the sinner
    who has received mercy there
  and is deemed worthy to be given access
    to the environs of Paradise;

---

[1]Gen. 25:26.

even though he remains outside,
    he may pasture there through grace.
As I reflected I was fearful again
    because I had presumed
to suppose that there might be
    between the Garden and the fire
a place where those who have found mercy
    can receive chastisement and forgiveness.

15. Praise to the Just One
    who rules with His grace;
He is the Good One who never draws in
    the limits of His goodness;
even to the wicked
    He stretches forth in His compassion.
His divine cloud hovers over
    all that is His;
it drips dew even on that fire of punishment
    so that, of His mercy,
it enables even the embittered
    to taste of the drops of its refreshment.

HYMN XI

Paradise can only be described in terrestrial terms, but it is essential to realize that these terms are purely metaphorical; to understand them in a literal sense is to abuse God's great condescension in revealing to us, through Scripture, something of Paradise's beauty and wonders. Yet, although Paradise belongs to a different mode of existence, outside time and space, it is still able to serve as a direct source of well-being for life on earth, a fact that the Genesis narrative expresses by means of the imagery of the fountain which issues forth from Paradise and divides itself up into the four great rivers of the world. Nowhere on earth was the fragrant breath of Paradise more

evident than in the Upper Chamber where the Apostles were
assembled at Pentecost.

1. The air of Paradise
        is a fountain of delight
    from which Adam sucked
        when he was young;
    its very breath, like a mother's breast,
        gave him nourishment in his childhood.
    He was young, fair,
        and full of joy,
    but when he spurned the injunction
        he grew old, sad and decrepit;
    he bore old age
        as a burden of woes.

RESPONSE: Blessed is He who exalted Adam
               and caused him to return to Paradise.

2. No harmful frost,
        no scorching heat
    is to be found
        in that blessed place of delight;
    it is a harbor of joys,
        a haven of pleasures;
    light and rejoicing
        have their home there;
    gathered there are to be found
        harps and lyres,
    with shouts of Hosanna,
        and the Church crying "Alleluia."

3. The fence which surrounds it
        is the peace which gives peace to all;

its inner and outer walls
    are the concord which reconciles all things;
the cherub who encircles it
    is radiant to those who are within
but full of menace to those outside
    who have been cast out.
All that you hear told
    about this Paradise,
so pure and holy,
    is pure and spiritual.

4. Let not this description of it
    be judged by one who hears it,
for descriptions of it
    are not at all subject to judgment,
since, even though it may appear terrestrial
    because of the terms used,
it is in its reality
    spiritual and pure.
Even though the name of "spirit"
    is applied to two kinds of beings,
yet the unclean spirit is quite separate
       from the one that is sanctified.

5. For him who would tell of it
    there is no other means
but to use the names
    of things that are visible,
thus depicting for his hearers
    a likeness of things that are hidden.
For if the Creator
    of the Garden
has clothed His majesty
    in terms that we can understand,
how much more can His Garden
    be described with our similes?

6. If someone concentrates his attention solely
        on the metaphors used of God's majesty,
    he abuses and misrepresents that majesty
        and thus errs
    by means of those metaphors
        with which God clothed Himself for his benefit,
    and he is ungrateful to that Grace
        which stooped low
    to the level of his childishness;
        although it has nothing in common with him,
    yet Grace clothed itself in his likeness
        in order to bring him to the likeness of itself.

7. Do not let your intellect
        be disturbed by mere names,
    for Paradise has simply clothed itself
        in terms that are akin to you;
    it is not because it is impoverished
        that it has put on your imagery;
    rather, your nature is far too weak
        to be able
    to attain to its greatness,
        and its beauties are much diminished
    by being depicted in the pale colors
        with which you are familiar.

8. For feeble eyes
        cannot gaze upon
    the dazzling sight
        of its celestial beauties;
    it has clothed its trees
        with the names of the trees we know;
    its figs are called
        by the same name as our figs,
    its leaves, which are spiritual,
        have taken on bodily form;

they have been changed
   so that their vesture may resemble ours.

9. More numerous and glorious
      than the stars
   in the sky that we behold
      are the blossoms of that land,
   and the fragrance which exhales from it
      through divine Grace
   is like a physician
      sent to heal the ills
   of a land that is under a curse;
      by its healing breath it cures
   the sickness that entered in
      through the serpent.

10. The breath that wafts
       from some blessed corner of Paradise
    gives sweetness
       to the bitterness of this region,
    it tempers the curse
       on this earth of ours.
    That Garden is
       the life-breath
    of this diseased world
       that has been so long in sickness;
    that breath proclaims that a saving remedy
       has been sent to heal our mortality.

11. What need was there
       that from that land
    a river should flow forth
       and divide itself,[1]

---

[1]Gen. 2:10.

except that the blessing of Paradise
　　should be mingled by means of water
as it issues forth
　　to irrigate the world,
making clean its fountains
　　that had become polluted by curses
—just as that "sickly water"
　　had been made wholesome by the salt.[2]

12. Thus it is with another spring,*
　　　full of perfumes,
　　which issues from Eden
　　　and penetrates into the atmosphere
　　as a beneficial breeze
　　　by which our souls are stirred;
　　our inhalation is healed
　　　by this healing breath
　　from Paradise;
　　　springs receive a blessing
　　from that blessed spring
　　　which issues forth from there.

13. A vast censer
　　　exhaling fragrance
　　impregnates the air
　　　with its odoriferous smoke,
　　imparting to all who are near it
　　　a whiff from which to benefit.
　　How much the more so
　　　with Paradise the glorious:
　　even its fence assists us,
　　　modifying somewhat
　　that curse upon the earth
　　　by the scent of its aromas.

---

[2] Kings 2:21.

14. When the blessed Apostles
      were gathered together[3]
   the place shook
      and the scent of Paradise,*
   having recognized its home,
      poured forth its perfumes,
   delighting the heralds
      by whom
   the guests are instructed
      and come to His banquet;
   eagerly He awaits their arrival
      for He is the Lover of mankind.

15. Make me worthy through Your grace
      to attain to Paradise's gift
   —this treasure of perfumes,
      this storehouse of scents.
   My hunger takes delight
      in the breath of its fragrance,
   for its scent gives nourishment to all
      at all times,
   and whoever inhales it
      is overjoyed and forgets his earthly bread;
   this is the table of the Kingdom—[4]
      blessed is He who prepared it in Eden.

HYMN XII

Truth can be put to deceptive use: the serpent promised Adam and Eve something that would have been true had they remained obedient to God's commandment, but by presuming to transgress the commandment and to snatch at what was

---

[3]cf Acts 2:1-4.
[4]Luke 22:30.

promised, all they gained was an awareness and knowledge of
what they had lost. Adam's fate thus resembled that of King
Uzziah who, by trying to seize the priesthood, lost the kingship
as well. Satan tried the same tactics with the second Adam,
quoting a psalm which indeed contained truth, but he did so
with deceptive intent. This time, however, it is the deceiver
who is deceived, and it is his deception that Christ rejects. The
demonic Legion, on the other hand, who begs Christ without
deception, is granted his request—a precedent which embold-
ens St Ephrem in making his own request.

Satan's deceptive use of Scripture is then contrasted with
Christ's beneficial use of actions which on the surface appear
negative or destructive. Indeed, from the very first all that
God does is aimed at the enhancement of the glory of humanity, the culmination of His creation: having created Adam and
Eve with free will, God wished them to win the crown of
immortality through their use of it, and so he hedged the Tree
of Knowledge about with the commandment not to eat of its
fruit. Failure to use this gift of free will reduces someone to
the lower status of the animals—whereas the animals, had they
but discernment, would bewail their not having been created
human beings!

1. There sprang up within me a query
          that troubled my thoughts;
    I wished to make enquiry,
          but was afraid of being importunate.
    But the moment God perceived
          what lay in my thoughts
    He enveloped with His wisdom
          this question of mine,
    and thus I felt assured
          that in all that He told me
    He had accepted my wish
          and encompassed it for me within His own words.

RESPONSE: Praise to Your grace that has compassion
                    on sinners.

2. For He explained to me
     about the serpent,
   how the truth concerning hidden things
     had reached this deceiver.
   It was by listening that he learned
     and imagined he had knowledge;[1]
   the voice had cried out
     to Adam and warned him
   of that Tree of knowledge
     of what is good and what evil;
   the cunning one heard that voice
     and seized on its meaning.

3. He deceived the husbandman
     so that he plucked prematurely
   the fruit which gives forth its sweetness
     only in due season
   —a fruit that, out of season,
     proves bitter to him who plucks it.
   Through a ruse did the serpent
     reveal the truth,
   knowing well that the result
     would be the opposite, because of their
     presumption;
   for blessing becomes a curse
     to him who seizes it in sin.

4. Remember Uzziah,
     how he entered the sanctuary;
   by seeking to seize the priesthood
     he lost his kingdom.[2]
   Adam, by wishing to enrich himself,
     incurred a double loss.

---

[1]Gen. 3:4-5.
[2]cf 2 Chron. 26:16-21.

Recognize in the sanctuary
    the Tree,
in the censer the fruit,
    and in the leprosy the nakedness.
From these two treasures
    there proceeded harm in both cases.

5. Abraham doubted and asked
      "How shall I know?"[3]
    He uttered what he wanted
      but found what he did not want.
    God, through a few brief words,
      taught him one thing in place of another.
    The same happened to Adam
      in the Garden:
    he lost what he had desired,
      and found what he dreaded:
    it was disgrace, instead of glory,
      that God caused the audacious man to know.

6. There came another Athlete,*
      this time not to be beaten;
    He put on the same armor
      in which Adam had been vanquished.
    When the adversary beheld
      the armor of conquered Adam,
    he rejoiced, not perceiving
      that he was being taken by surprise;
    He who was within the armor would have terrified
    him,
      but His exterior gave him courage.
    The evil one came to conquer,
      but he was conquered and could not hold his
      ground.

---

[3]Gen. 15:8.

7. Observe how there too
    the evil one revealed the truth:
   he recited Scripture there,
    he exacted truth there;
   he clothed himself* with a psalm,[4]
    hoping to win by reciting it.
   But our Lord would not listen
    to him—
   not because what he said
    was untrue,
   but because the evil one
    had armed himself with deception.

8. Look too at Legion:[5]
    when in anguish he begged,
   our Lord permitted and allowed him
    to enter into the herd;
   respite did he ask for, without deception,
    in his anguish,
   and our Lord in His kindness
    granted this request.
   His compassion for demons
    is a rebuke to that People,*
   showing how much anguish His love suffers
    in desiring that men and women should live.

9. Encouraged by the words
    I had heard,
   I knelt down and wept there,
    and spoke before our Lord:
   "Legion received his request from You
    without any tears;
   permit me, with my tears,
    to make my request,

---

[4]Matt. 4:6 (quoting Ps. 90(91): 11).
[5]Mark 5:9.

grant me to enter, instead of that herd,
  the Garden,
so that in Paradise I may sing
  of its Planter's compassion.

10. Because Adam touched the Tree
       he had to run to the fig;
     he became like the fig tree,
       being clothed in its vesture:
     Adam, like some tree,
       blossomed with leaves.*
     Then he came to that glorious
       tree of the Cross,
     put on glory from it,
       acquired radiance from it,
     heard from it the truth
       that he would return to Eden once more.[6]

11. Let Job uncover for you
       the impudence of Satan:[7]
     how he asks and beseeches
       the Just One for permission
     to test out your minds
       in the furnace of temptation.
     This is what
       the abominable one said:
     "No silver without fire
       has ever been assayed;
     falsehood will be put to shame,
       what is true will receive due praise.

12. It is written, furthermore,
       Show no favor to the rich,

_____

[6]Luke 23:43.
[7]cf Job 1:9-11.

do not even help out
a poor man in court;[8]
let not judgment be blinded
in the eye of the scales
so that truth may be apparent
in all things;
if it is a case of forgiveness,
let us praise His grace,
if of punishment,
let us acknowledge His justice."

13. Our Lord rebuked the demon
and shut his mouth;[9]
He was angry with the leper,
He said "woe" to the scribes[10]
along with the rich;
the swine He cast into the sea,[11]
He dried up
the fig tree.*[12]
But all these were occasions
for us to receive benefit,
for by their means He opened up
the great gates of His discerning actions.

14. He did not use threats,
but gave a rebuke in order to save;
even though He said "woe,"
yet His nature is peaceable,
even though He rebuked the demon,
He remains completely serene;

---

[8]cf Lev. 19:15.
[9]Mark 1:25.
[10]Mark 1:43; Matt. 23:13.
[11]Luke 6:24; Matt. 8:32.
[12]Matt. 21:19.

it was not out of anger
   that He bade the swine
be cast into the sea;
   nor was it hate which withered up
the fig at His curse,
   for He is in all things good.

15. Two Trees did God place
     in Paradise,
   the Tree of Life
     and that of Wisdom,[13]
   a pair of blessed fountains,
     source of every good;
   by means of this
     glorious pair
   the human person can become
     the likeness of God,
   endowed with immortal life
     and wisdom that does not err.

16. With that manifest knowledge
     which God gave to Adam,
   whereby he gave names to Eve
     and to the animals,[14]
   God did not reveal the discoveries
     of things that were concealed;
   but in the case
     of that hidden knowledge
   from the stars downward,
     Adam was able to pursue
   enquiry into all
     that is within this universe.

---

[13]Gen. 2:9.
[14]Gen. 2:20, 3:20.

17. For God would not grant him the crown
    without some effort;
He placed two crowns for Adam,
    for which he was to strive,
two Trees to provide crowns
    if he were victorious.
If only he had conquered
    just for a moment,
he would have eaten the one and lived,
    eaten the other and gained knowledge;
his life would have been protected from harm
    and his wisdom would have been unshakable.

18. The Just One did not wish
    to give Adam the crown quite free,
even though He had allowed him
    to enjoy Paradise without toil;
God knew that if Adam wanted
    he could win the prize.
The Just One ardently wished
    to enhance him,
for, although the rank of supernal beings
    is great through grace,
the crown for the proper use of free will
    is by no means paltry.

19. In His justice He gave
    abundant comfort to the animals;
they do not feel shame for adultery,
    nor guilt for stealing;
without being ashamed
    they pursue every comfort they encounter,
for they are above
    care and shame;
the satisfaction of their desires
    is sufficient to please them.

Because they have no resurrection,
    neither are they subject to blame.

20. The fool, who is unwilling to realize
        his honorable state,
    prefers to become just an animal,
        rather than a man,
    so that, without incurring judgment,
        he may serve naught but his lusts.
    But had there been sown in animals
        just a little
    of the sense of discernment,
        then long ago would the wild asses have lamented
    and wept at their not
        having been human.

HYMN XIII

Picking up the theme on which Hymn XII ends, St Ephrem
compares the fallen Adam to King Nebuchadnezzar, whose
rebellion against God (Daniel 4) led to his becoming like a
wild animal. The fact that Nebuchadnezzar returned to his
kingdom once he had repented gives hope to us and encourages
us too to repent in order that we may return to the kingdom
from which Adam/humanity had been expelled. But whereas
Nebuchadnezzar abhorred his place of exile, we have become
so inured to sin that we actually take pleasure in our exile and
have to be rescued from it against our perverted wills; in this
we are rebuked by the examples of Samson, Jonah and Joseph,
who all rejoiced in their deliverance, whereas we lament when
any of us pass from this life to the next.

1. Let me speak what is needful,
        teach what may be heard,

seek what may be attained,
  spurn all that is inquisitive;
may I ask only what is useful for me,
  and speak what befits You,
both what is needful
  and what is necessary.
May I take what Grace proffers
  and give the thanksgiving that is appropriate;
through Your grace may my offering
  enter before Your good pleasure.

RESPONSE: Through Your grace make me worthy
           of that Garden of happiness.

2. In the beginning God created the creation,
      the fountainhead of delights;
    the house which He constructed
      provisions those who live therein,
    for upon His gift
      innumerable created beings depend;
    from a single table
      does He provide
    every day for each creature
      all things in due measure.
    Grant that we may acknowledge
      Your grace, O Good One.

3. A garden full of glory,
      a chaste bridal chamber,
    did he give to that king*
      fashioned from the dust,
    sanctifying and separating him
      from the abode of wild animals;
    for glorious was Adam
      in all things—

in where he lived and what he ate,
   in his radiance and dominion.
Blessed is He who elevated him above all
   so that he might give thanks to the Lord of all.

4. The king of Babylon resembled[1]
      Adam king of the universe:
   both rose up against the one Lord
      and were brought low;
   He made them outlaws,
      casting them afar.
   Who can fail to weep,
      seeing that these free-born kings
   preferred slavery
      and servitude.
   Blessed is He who released us
      so that His image might no longer be in bondage.

5. David wept for Adam,[2]
      at how he fell
   from that royal abode
      to the abode of wild animals.
   Because he went astray through a beast
      he became like the beasts:
   He ate, together with them
      as a result of the curse,
   grass and roots,
      and he died, becoming their peer.
   Blessed is He who set him apart
      from the wild animals* again.

6. In that king*
      did God depict Adam:

---

[1] cf Dan. 4.
[2] cf Ps. 48(49):13.

since he provoked God by his exercise of kingship,
    God stripped him of that kingship.
The Just One was angry and cast him out
    into the region of wild beasts;
he dwelt there with them
    in the wilderness[3]
and only when he repented did he return
    to his former abode and kingship.
Blessed is He who has thus taught us to repent
    so that we too may return to Paradise.

7. Because it was not easy
    for us to see our fallen state—
how and whence we had fallen
    at the very outset—
He depicted it all together
    in that king,
portraying in our fall
    his fall,
and portraying our return
    in his repentant return.
Praise to Him who delineated
    this likeness for the repentant.

8. Although he disliked
    the abode of wild beasts
it was necessary
    for the king to remain there;
yet, despite his madness and error,
    he recalled that he was a man
and prayed that he might be returned
    to his own former abode;
and when the Good One returned him,
    he gave thanks to Him for His compassion.

[3]Dan. 4:32-3.

Blessed is He who gave us in him
  an example of returning.

9. Look at how great is our shame
    in comparison:
  our very confinement in darkness
    has become for us a source of pleasure;
  we are proud
    of the land of curses;[4]
  how we love
    our confinement in a pit!
  Like the Egyptians
    we are drowned in the sea.[5]
  Blessed is He who has had pity on us
    so that we should not be left in this our state.

10. The Good One in His love
    wished to discipline us for doing wrong,
  and so we had to leave Paradise
    with its bridal chamber of glory;
  He made us live with the wild beasts,
    which caused us sorrow,
  so that we might see how little
    our honor had become,
  and so would supplicate Him and beg to return
    to our inheritance.
  Praise be to Him who released
    these prisoners who have no wish to be free![6]

11. In both his mind and understanding
    was the king of Babylon childlike,
  but through our Lord, my brethren,
    your understanding is complete.

[4]Gen. 3:17.
[5]Exod. 14:28.
[6]cf Isaiah 61:1.

He returned to Babylon:[7]
  both he and the city have vanished;
but do you, my brothers,
  seek your city,*
for both you and it
  shall endure forever.
Happy are those who live there,
  for in it none ever need to be buried.

12. Satan the tyrant outwitted Samson
      with a woman,[8]
    the same tyrant outwitted Adam
      with a woman:
    Samson had to grind at the mill,[9]
      Adam had to labor wearily on the soil;
    Samson prayed
      to be released,
    whereas we pray
      to grow old in our misery.
    Blessed is He who delivered Samson,
      releasing him from the grinding.

13. Samson is a type of the death
      of Christ the High Priest:
    Samson's death returns prisoners
      to their towns,[10]
    whereas the High Priest's death
      has returned us to our heritage.
    Let us repeat to each other
      the good news in joy,
    that the gate is once again open,
      and happy is he who enters in quickly.

---

[7]Dan. 4:36.
[8]Judges 16.
[9]Judges 16:21.
[10]cf Judges 16:23-31.

Blessed is He who has not made us
   outlaws never to return.

14. Jonah knew into what
        the Just One had cast him;
     he prayed, and was brought back to land.[11]
        In him we shall be judged, my brothers,
     for we do not even realize
        whither we have been driven out.
     Jonah came up from the whale and gave thanks:
        he was not ungrateful;
     but we think it a cause for complaint
        when we are released from our yoke.
     Yet You, Lord, put up with us,
        who complain as we are rescued.

15. Joseph took no delight,
        despite all the honor that was paid him,
     in remaining in prison;[12]
        his example rebukes us, my brothers,
     for the more we are in bondage,
        the more we are pleased.
     He was released, and reached his true stature,
        in order to teach us
     how, in the Kingdom, our departed ones too
        achieve their full stature:
     being separated from us for a little,
        they have come to their Lord,

16. This day of separation,
        which to us seems to cut off all hope,
     only increases their hope,
        now that they are returning to their own city:

---

[11]Jonah 2.
[12]Gen. 41:14.

lamentation for those below,
   but joy for those above;
the world below sorrows at the loss
   of their familiar voices,
but the heaven above is overjoyed
   that their song is now intermingled with the
   song of the seraphs.
Blessed is the man who weeps over himself,
   rather than for the departed.

HYMN XIV

St Ephrem continues both the alphabetic acrostic and the theme of the previous hymn: in our failure to recognize our captive state on earth we resemble the Hebrew slave who preferred continued slavery to the freedom to which he was entitled after seven years' service. Our misguided love for our present condition is rebuked by the examples of numerous Old Testament saints: all of them urge us to seek our true city in Eden. Particularly illogical are our laments over the deaths of children who now pasture in Paradise; humanity is in fact like a tree from which fruit is daily plucked as an offering. And what is most remarkable of all is that the unripe fruit—those who die young—is even sweeter than the ripe!

1. All of us each day in many diverse ways
   are under constraint
to learn by experience
   not to be held captive here upon earth,
yet despite this experience
   our minds remain down below.
Blessed is that person who has realized
   how worthwhile it is
to lay in provisions
   for receiving our Lord;

blessed indeed is he at whose merchandise
    his Lord is pleased.

RESPONSE: Grant us to welcome Your kingdom
            with cries of "Hosanna."

2. How much we resemble
        the slave who rejected
    the liberty offered him
        by the seventh year:
    he allowed his ear to be pierced,
        becoming a slave in perpetuity.[1]
    It is liberty that they receive
        at their death,
    those weary ones whom you have buried,
        the chaste whose coffin you have followed.

3. Jeremiah was thrown into a pit[2]
        that proved beneficial;
    yet, though his reward was great,
        he had no desire to tarry there.
    But we, whose life here on earth
        is blended with all kinds of ills,
    still pray that we may be
        allowed to remain here,
    for we do not perceive
        how we are being strangled.
    O Lord, grant that we may recognize
        the place where we are held prisoner.

4. We should learn from Daniel,[3]
        who prayed

[1]Exod. 21:2, 5.
[2]cf Jer. 37:15-16; 38:6.
[3]cf Dan. 9:15-19.

that he might come up from Babylon
 to the land of promise;
Babylon is the likeness of this earth,
 full of curses.
God gave us this type which He depicted
 so that we too
might pray that we return
 to our dwelling in Eden.
Blessed is He who brings us forth
 through grace to our goal.

5. Noah too, in a mystery,
 expectantly prayed
to be released
 from the ark and to go forth,[4]
even though there was nothing within it
 to cause him any harm.
How much more should we
 turn our backs
on this abode,
 this harbor of misfortunes.
Blessed is that person who has steered
 his boat straight into Paradise.

6. Moses in Egypt
 was held in great honor:
Pharoah's daughter called him her own son[5]
 —yet rejecting this,
he chose to be just a shepherd,[6]
 living in hardship.
How much more should we
 rejoice at our departure

4cf Gen. 8:6-12.
5Exod. 2:10, Heb. 11:24.
6Exod. 3:1.

when we are released from this place of servitude
   and discover our liberty.
Blessed is that person
   who finds freedom in Paradise.

7. Jacob led out his sheep
   and brought them to his father's home;[7]
a symbol for those with discernment,
   a parable for those with perception
is to be found in this homecoming:
   let us too return to our Father's house,[8]
my brethren, and not become
   captivated with desire
for this transient earth
   —for your true city is in Eden.[9]
Blessed indeed is that person
   who has seen his dear ones in its midst.

8. There all fruit is holy,
   all raiment luminous,
every crown glorious,
   every rank the most exalted—
happiness without toil,
   delight that knows no fear,
a marriage feast which continues
   for ever and ever.
By contrast, to my eyes this abode
   seems one of torment:
blessed the person who says
   "Lord, release me from here."

9. To the voices of the celestial beings,
   to the melody of the spiritual,

---

[7]Gen. 31:17.
[8]cf Luke 15:20.
[9]cf Philipp. 3:20, Hebr. 11:16.

to the seraphs with their chants,
  to the cherubs with their wings:
to all their lovely music
  there is no comparison here below.
Their delight is in
  the praise which they render,
each one receiving
  rich sustenance through his lyre.
Make us worthy to take delight, along with them,
  in cries of "Hosanna."

10. If we momentarily throw aside
      the veil from our eyes
    and glance at that place,
      we will rue our delay
    which we have prolonged in this world,
      the harbor of debts,*
    where merchants each day
      suffer great loss,
    where ships are wrecked
      and cargoes are seized.
    Blessed are the children
      who have passed through it without toil.

11. In Paradise these sheep
      may pasture without fear,
    while Satan laments
      that he has left no mark on them;
    lust too is downcast,
      not having stained them,
    but virginity rejoices
      as she reigns
    in these chaste temples
      that were in no wise sullied.
    Happy the person held worthy to reach
      their place of meeting.

12. Their beauty never fades,
         their radiance never dims;
     their parents will regret
         their misguided recriminations
     and give thanks, once they are there,
         to Him whom they decried here below.
     Yes, they will thank
         the Gracious One who endures
     our wailing lamentation
         and all our rent garments.
     Blessed is He who, despite our provocation,
         has brought to true stature those whom we love.

13. Praise to the Husbandman*
         who tends the tree of humanity,
     who plucks off each day
         fruit to serve as an offering
     —fruits of all sizes,
         kinds and varieties;
     and what is so wonderful,
         the unripe fruits
     are even sweeter
         than those that have ripened.
     Blessed is He who has offered up to His Father
         a crown of young children.

14. There remorse overtakes
         the many people
     who were tested and did not persevere,
         who were chastened and did not sustain it;
     the Good One chose
         only small and transient punishments
     to wipe out their bill of debt,[10]
         but they would have none of it:

---

[10]Col. 2:14.

because they found fault with Grace,
now in justice they feel remorse.
Praise to You from all,
for You are entirely good to all.

15. May Your grace bring me too back,
who am held in captivity;
my forefathers were taken away captive
from the Garden of Eden
to this land of thorns
through Satan's ill counsel;
it was he who has beguiled me
into dearly loving
this land of curses,
this place of chastisement.
Blessed is He who has brought us back from captivity
and slain him who took us away captive.

HYMN XV

Paradise can be compared to the wind: although it cannot be seen, it is nonetheless experienced. The Tree of Knowledge —awareness of truth and of spiritual reality—is the gate to Paradise, through which the mind can enter. But the Tree of Knowledge has to be approached in the right spirit and in obedience to God; otherwise, it will lead to destruction and loss, as both Adam and Uzziah discovered. Furthermore, once led astray by eating the fruit of the Tree in disobedience, man goes on to blame the fruit, rather than his greed for the consequences of his grasping. So strong indeed was the serpent's poison that it enabled Satan to turn aside (the verb is *sta* in Syriac, providing a word play) the whole of humanity—when we should be listening instead to another representative of the animal world, the ass whose brief words to Balaam saved its master from destruction.

1. My brethren, consider the wind:
        though its blast is tumultuous,
    it lacks any color by which it can be seen,
        for it is hidden in its manifestation;
    having no outer array
        or substance at all,
    it is both hidden and yet manifest
        when it is blowing.
    So too the abode of Paradise
        is both hidden and manifest:
    while it can be perceived to exist,
        what it really is cannot be perceived.

RESPONSE: Blessed is He who came and invited
                both worlds to His Paradise.

2. The tree that is called
        the Tree of Knowledge
    symbolizes the gate
        of Paradise:
    it is through the gate of knowledge
        that one is able to enter in;
    it is the likeness
        of its glorious Creator,
    in whose hidden abode
        through the gate of knowledge
    all who are perceptive
        may approach His hiddenness.

3. Consider this knowledge
        which is the gateway to all things:
    by it the intellect
        can enter everywhere,
    though where it meets error
        in front of it

it comes up against a wall
  and is blocked.
Through this gate of knowledge
  the intellect enters in,
explores every kind of treasure,
  brings out every kind of riches.

4. Even when the army
     surrounded Elisha
   a voice proved the key
     to the eyes of the shepherd.[1]
   When the disciple's eyes
     were held closed,
   bread too was the key
     whereby their eyes were opened
   to recognize the Omniscient:[2]
     saddened eyes beheld
   a vision of joy
     and were instantly filled with happiness.

5. So likewise that Wood,
     which is the Tree of Knowledge,
   can, with its fruit, roll back
     the cloud of ignorance,
   so that eyes can recognize
     the beauty
   of that Tabernacle
     hidden within;
   but because Adam and Eve
     ate it in sin,
   the vision that should have caused joy of heart
     resulted in grief of heart.

---

[1] 2 Kings 6:17.
[2] Luke 24:31.

6. Intelligence is
        like a treasurer
    who carries on his shoulder[3]
        the keys to learning,*
    fitting a key
        to each locked door,
    opening with ease
        even the most difficult—
    skilled in what is manifest,
        well instructed in what is hidden,
    training souls
        and enriching creation.

7. The precious stones of the ephod
        worn by the priest in accord with the
        commandment
    he called
        "luminous" and "perfect,"*
    as well as
        "knowledge" and "truth."[4]
    Thus the priest was robed in knowledge
        whereby he might hear
    the voice that came to him
        from inside the sanctuary,
    for it spoke to him
        from between the cherubim.

8. Accompanied by the knowledge
        which was hidden in the ephod
    the priest entered the sanctuary,
        a type for Paradise,
    and he tasted of the Tree
        through the symbol of the revelation given him.

---

[3]cf Isaiah 22:22.
[4]Exod. 28:30; Lev. 8:8.

But if anyone entered
    contrary to the commandment, they died,
as a type of Adam who died
    for taking the fruit prematurely.
The priest put on sanctification,
    but Adam was stripped of glory.*

9. The intellect cannot explore
        the bosom of those trees
    without that fruit,
        nor can the priest investigate
    that treasury of revelations
        without the ephod.
    Two people did the evil one beguile and captivate
        with his blandishments—
    promising to make Adam into a god
        and Uzziah into a priest,[5]
    whereas in reality he stripped the one of his glory
        and clothed the other in leprosy.

10. The Exalted One gave to Adam
        the luxury of Paradise
    and to Uzziah
        the luxury of kingship.
    To the former he forbade the fruit,
        to the latter the censer.
    Both however grasped at
        something they were not given:
    with the censer
        Uzziah's name turned putrid,
    with the scented fruit
        Adam's name became loathsome.

11. It is easy to understand
        how mankind

---

[5] 2 Chron. 26:16-21.

has come to hate creation:
  having become hateful themselves, they hold
  creation to be hateful;
by sacrificing flesh they spoil it,
  by defiling marriage they have set it aside,
while gold they make hateful
  by means of their idols.
Since it was through the fair fruit
  that Adam became odious
he has made that fruit an object of hate,
  considering it to be harmful.

12. It is obvious that the censer
  of the inner sanctuary is good,
but the Tree in Paradise
  has come to be considered as poisonous.
If the censer is glorious,
  then the fruit is even more so;
through the censer, pure and glorious,
  the evil one
made royalty leprous,
  and likewise in Paradise
the cunning one slew
  the young couple with the excellent fruit.

13. Of the serpent
  which spoke for a moment
God provided an illustration
  in the speech of the ass[6]
which spoke for a moment
  to rebuke the audacious Balaam.
So too the serpent spoke
  in order to test

---

[6]Num. 22:28.

the ears of Adam and Eve:
  their ears heard two voices,
and at the voice of the bitter one
  they held the Sweet One's to be false.

14. The serpent served as a garment
       for the evil one to put on:
  on seeing the innocent ones
     he became full of guile,
  he prepared a cunning trap
     for the hearing of the young couple.
  In their simplicity
     they listened to his words eagerly,
  for he made a show of his care,
     but hid well his guile.
  On another occasion the Iscariot
     can instruct you in the devil's types.

15. How strong is his poison,
       upsetting the whole world.
  Who can hold back the sea
     of that bitter one?
  Everyone contains drops of it
     that can harm you.
  Judas was the treasurer[7]
     of his poison,
  and although Satan's form is hidden,
     in Judas he is totally visible;
  though Satan's history is a long one,
     it is summed up in the Iscariot.

16. Let the ass put the serpent to shame
       with its brief words:
  it spoke the truth,
     while from the serpent issued falsehood;

---

[7]John 12:6.

it turned aside to turn away greedy Balaam
   who had gone awry.[8]
The serpent too turned aside,*
   and caused us to go aside to our destruction;
it made crooked our thoughts,
   and so God made crooked its path;
the course it travels
   indicates how it turned awry our road.

17. All this, and similar things
   that I have read in the Scriptures,
have helped depict in my mind
   that Garden of Life;
blessed is the person who is worthy to attain
   its enjoyment.
May the Merciful One
   bring me to its fruits,
may their taste give me life,
   or their scent strike me,
or their radiance reach me,
   or their dew bathe me!

---

[8]Num. 22:23.

Notes to the Hymns on Paradise

(Marked with asterisks in the text)

I.1   *master*: or "teacher" (*rabbā*), perhaps reflecting Jewish usage, *Mōshē rabbēnū*, "Moses our teacher."
Law: Ephrem uses the archaic term *urāytā*, of Jewish Aramaic origin, rather than the more usual *nāmōsā*, from Greek *nomos*. The term *urāytā* deliberately associates the Hebrew word Torah, Law, with the root *'wr*, "light."

I.6   *bridal chambers*: for the importance of this theme see the Introduction.

I.10   *valley*: for the topography of Paradise and its surroundings see the Introduction.
Qardu: Ephrem follows the Syriac Bible which, together with Josephus and the Targumim, identifies the mountain where the Ark came to rest as Mt Qardu in North Iraq, rather than Mt Ararat in Armenia.

I.11   *sons of God*: Gen. 6:2. Several interpretations of this term were current in antiquity; the Septuagint paraphrased the Hebrew with "angels," and the Book of Enoch links the passage with the idea of fallen angels who intermarried with mankind. Ephrem, however, follows a quite different tradition, first attested by Julius Africanus (c. 160-c. 240), according to which the "sons of God" were the Sethites, who dwelt on higher ground, while the "daughters of men" were the Cainites, who lived lower down. This interpretation, known to several of the Greek Fathers (see L. R. Wickhan in *Oudtestamentische Studien* 19 (1974), pp. 135-47) became the standard one in the Syriac Church (a detailed exposition of the tradition is to be found in section III of Ephrem's *Commentary on Genesis*).

I.13   *a mother . . .*: perhaps Ephrem has in mind a particular instance.

I.16   *but if*: Ephrem deliberately leaves the sentence without a main clause.

I.16   *crumbs*: an allusion to Matt. 15:27, in the narrative of Christ and the Canaanite woman. Compare VII.26 and IX.29.

I.17   *begs for succor*: both Ephrem and Aphrahat used a Biblical text (probably the Diatessaron) where *parakaleitai* in Luke 16:25 was translated, not by "[Lazarus] is comforted," but "is supplicated"—that is, by the Rich Man. Compare also Ephrem's *Letter to Publius,* section 4 (edition and translation in *Le Muséon* 89 (1976)).

II   Response: The lance which pierced the side of Christ is regularly contrasted typologically with the sword of the cherub guarding Paradise (see the Introduction). The refrain to VI expresses the same idea more obliquely ("Blessed is He who through His Cross has flung open Paradise for us").

II.2   *key*: Ephrem employs this imagery again at III.5, VI.1, VII.1, VIII.2 and XV.4 and 6.

II.3   *. . . your inheritance, darkness*: not a direct Biblical quotation, but compare Matt. 8:12ff; Luke 12:16-20.

II.4   *their luxurious living* (*nyāhā*): there is probably a double entendre here, for *nyāhā* can refer either to their former "luxurious living," or to the "rest," or "peace of mind," that they might have enjoyed in Paradise.

II.7   *boundary . . . garments*: for these themes see the Introduction.

II.8   *issue forth toward us*: Ephrem refers to the four rivers of Gen. 2:10, whose geographical relationship to the Paradise mountain is explained in his Commentary on Genesis II.6 (see the translation below).

II.11   *God's Presence*: Ephrem uses the Syriac form of the Jewish term *Shekhina* here.

III.6   *Their eyes were opened*: compare Commentary on Genesis II.21-2.

III.8   *that hero of old*: an allusion to Tantalus. A further allusion to classical mythology can be found in the Nisibene Hymns XXXVI.5 (Orpheus).

III.12   *Had Adam conquered*: compare Commentary on Genesis II.23.

III.14   *Uzziah*: Ephrem frequently refers to this king who tried to usurp the role of priest as well (II Chron. 26); in the Paradise Hymns see XII.4 and XV.9-10.
  both kings: Ephrem and the Syriac Fathers follow Rabbinic tradition which regarded Adam as both king and priest; compare XIII.3-4.

III.15   *deprived of its feet*: the serpent was punished by the loss of its feet (deduced from Gen. 3:14) according to a Jewish tradition also known to Aphrahat (Demonstration IX.8 and XIV 12); see for example Josephus, *Antiquities* I, 50 (further references can be found in Kronholm, p. 113, note 72).

IV.5   *another robe*: the thought is densely packed here: the robe is the "robe of glory" which Christ has once again made available for humanity (Adam), and the penitent thief is taken here as the first representative of the human race to re-enter Paradise in this robe; see also Introduction. For Eve-Mary typology in the early Syriac Fathers see R. Murray, "Mary the Second Eve in the early Syriac Fathers," *Eastern Churches Review* 3 (1971), pp. 372-84, and S. P. Brock, "Mary in Syriac Tradition," in A. Stacpoole (ed.), *Mary's Place in Christian Dialogue* (Slough, 1982), pp. 182-91.

IV.10   *little coin*: perhaps an allusion to Mark 12:42, but Ephrem is also depicting himself as a beggar.

V.1   *created things*: the manuscripts offer two different readings here; in the *Harp of the Spirit* (no. 2) the other reading was adopted.

V.2   *witness to the Creator*: for Scripture and Nature as God's two witnesses (John 8:17) compare Hymns against the Heresies XXVIII.11:

> Look and see how Nature and Scripture
>   are yoked together for the Husbandman:
> Nature abhors adulterers,
>   practicers of magic and murderers;
>   Scripture abhors them too.
> Once Nature and Scripture had cleaned the land
>   they sowed in it new commandments

—in the land of the heart, so that it might bear fruit,
praise for the Lord of Nature
glory for the Lord of Scripture.

V.10   *heart*: according to Semitic anthropology, the heart
was the seat of the intellectual faculties as well as of
the emotions.

V.11   *empty*: since the final Resurrection, when the body and
soul would be reunited (and so enabled to enter Paradise: see Hymn VIII), had not yet taken place.

V.14   *splendors*: literally "luxuries," a term which Ephrem
will have derived (indirectly) from the Septuagint translation of "Eden" as *truphē*.

V.15   *diligent*: a word often used by Syriac writers in connection with the parable of the talents (Luke 19:11-27).
Compare also Hymn VI.11.

 VI   Response *flung open*: literally "breached," a verb
sometimes used by Ephrem for the action of the lance
in John 19:34.

VI.5   *rode*: literally "the vehicle (of the Son of its Lord)."
Ephrem uses this striking imagery on a number of
occasions, e.g. Hymns on Unleavened Bread XIII.8,
Hymns on Faith XVII.8.

VI.6   *plants*: the term often refers to medicinal herbs.

VI.8   *fruit*: the line implies that Communion was received
daily.

VI.9   *whitened*: i.e. at baptisms.

VI.12 *chaste (qaddīshē)*: for this technical term, referring
to the married who abstain from sexual intercourse,
see the Introduction.

VI.19 *Sheol*: the abode of the dead in the Hebrew Bible
(Septuagint "Hades").

VI.21 *from every quarter*: this may reflect Jewish speculation
of the Hellenistic period: in the Sibylline Books
(III.24-6) Adam's very name was held to signify that
he was created out of earth from the East (*anatolē*),
West (*dusis*), North (*arktos*) and South (*mesēmbria*).

VI.23 *Watchers*: i.e. angels; the term is taken from the Book
of Daniel.

VII.3 *life of mourning*: the "mourners" (*abīlē*, based on

Matt. 5:4) refer to those who had adopted a penitential way of life.

VII.7   *stripped off*: a deliberate irony, in view of Gen. 39:12.

VII.9   *first fruits*: compare XIV.13.

VII.11   *No blemish*: i.e. in Paradise.

VII.18   It has been claimed that this verse inspired the description of the *houris* of Paradise in the Koran; Beck, however, has shown that this hypothesis rests on a misunderstanding of the Syriac text (see Bibliographical Note).

VII.19   *seven sons of light*: the reference is to the seven Maccabaean martyrs, put to death at the order of King Antiochus before the very eyes of their mother (in 2 Macc. 7 she is unnamed, but later Jewish tradition knows her as Hannah, Syriac as Shmoni, and Greek as Solomone).

VII.21   *useless*: perhaps a reminiscence of Odes of Solomon 11:23, "For there is much space in Your Paradise, and there is nothing in it that is useless."

VII.24   *name*: of Christian.

IX.1   *paschal joy*: there is a play on words, for *mapsah* can mean either "give joy" or "celebrate passover."

IX.15   *Chaldeans*: famed in antiquity for their knowledge of astronomy and astrology.

X.3   *Eden's delights*: there is a word play in the Syriac.

XI.4   *heavenly*: the text can be vocalized either as *shmayānā* "heavenly," or as *shamīnā* "fecund."

X.5   *chaste*: see note to VI.12.

X.8   *buds*: the Syriac can also mean "wombs" (compare X.9).

XI.12   *another spring*: probably baptism is meant.

XI.14   *scent of Paradise*: several early Syriac writers refer to the fragrance experienced by the apostles at Pentecost, and it has been suggested that the lost Old Syriac version of Acts also contained such a reference.

XII.6   *Athlete*: this title is already applied to Christ in the Syriac Acts of Thomas (third century); cf R. Murray, *Symbols of Church and Kingdom* (Cambridge, 1975), p. 198.

XII.7   *clothed himself*: this metaphor is also frequently used

of the Incarnation. In the Nisibene hymns (XXXV.4)
Ephrem has Satan say:

> I lured Him [Christ] after His fast with excellent
>   bread
> —but He would have none of it;
> I struggled painfully to learn a psalm
> in order to catch Him by means of His own psalms:
> I took great care to learn my set piece,
> but He made this set piece of mine utterly ineffective.

XII.8   *People*: the Jewish People as opposed to the Gentile
         Peoples.

XII.10   *blossomed with leaves*: the same quaint image occurs
         in an early Byzantine acrostic hymn on Adam, stanza 8
         (P. Maas, *Frühbyzantinische Kirchenpoesie* (Berlin,
         1931), p. 14): "like a tree he wore fig leaves."

XII.13   *the fig tree*: in his Commentary on the Diatessaron
         Ephrem explains the incident of Matt. 21:20-1 as
         follows:

> When Adam sinned and was stripped of the glory
> in which he was clothed, he covered his nakedness
> with fig leaves. Our Savior came and underwent
> suffering in order to heal Adam's wounds and to
> provide a garment of glory for his nakedness. He
> dried up the fig tree in order to show that there
> would no longer be any need of fig leaves to serve
> as Adam's garment, since Adam had returned to
> his former glory, and so no longer had any need
> of leaves or "garments of skin."

XII.17-18 Compare the Commentary on Genesis II.17 (translated
           below).

XIII.3   *king*: i.e. Adam; see on II.14.

XIII.5   *from the wild animals*: a variant reading here has
         "from them at the Resurrection."

XIII.6   *that king*: i.e. Nebuchadnezzar (Dan. 4).

XIII.11 *city*: perhaps Ephrem alludes to Hebrews 11:16; com-
         pare hymn XIV.7.

XIV.10   *debts*: the context suggests that this is the correct read-
         ing (the other manuscript reads "harbor of joys").

XIV.13   *Husbandman*: a favorite divine title in Ephrem's writ-

ings: see R. Murray, *Symbols of Church and Kingdom*,
pp. 195-7.

XV.6   *learning*: or, perhaps, "doctrine"; cf VI.1.

XV.7   *"luminous" and "perfect"*: these are the Urim and
Thummim on the high priest's breast-piece; Ephrem
follows the Peshitta's rendering of these two Hebrew
terms (Exod. 28:30 "luminous and perfect"; Lev. 8:8
"knowledge and truth"; the Septuagint has "manifesta-
tion and truth" in both passages).

XV.8   A detailed discussion of this stanza is given by E. Beck
in *Oriens Christianus* 62 (1978), pp. 24-35.

XV.16   *turned aside*: the Syriac text has an elaborate word
play, for "Satan" was often derived by popular etymol-
ogy from *stā* "turned aside."

(The reader who would like a much more extensive commentary
on the Paradise Hymns is referred to E. Beck, *Ephraems Hymnen
über das Paradis* (*Studia Anselmiana* 26, 1951) and T. Kronholm,
*Motifs from Genesis 1-11 in the genuine Hymns of Ephrem the
Syrian* (*Coniectanea Biblica, Old Testament Series* 11; Lund, 1978),
pp. 45-134).

3.
THE COMMENTARY
ON GENESIS
(Section II)

ST EPHREM, COMMENTARY ON GENESIS,
Section II (Genesis 2-3)

Many of the themes in the Paradise Hymns find their best illustration in St Ephrem's own prose commentary on Genesis, whose second section covers chapters 2-3 of that Biblical book. Even though the beginning and end of this section of the commentary cover topics not alluded to in the Paradise Hymns, it has seemed preferable to offer a complete translation of it, rather than a series of excerpts.

1. After speaking about the Sabbath rest, and how God had blessed and sanctified this day, Scripture* returns to the narrative of the inital establishment of creation, this time passing over, with only a few words, things it had already spoken of* and recounting at greater length matters it had previously omitted. Thus it begins to describe the history of creation for a second time: "These are the generations of heaven and earth when they were created on the day that God made heaven and earth. None of the trees of the field was yet in existence, and the vegetation

had not yet sprouted, seeing that He had not yet caused rain to fall on the earth, and Adam was not there to work on the earth. A fountain went up and irrigated the surface of the earth."[1]

2. You should realize, reader, that even though the days of creation were completed and Scripture had pronounced a blessing on the Sabbath day that had been sanctified and had brought it to a close,[1] it now reverts to narrating the very beginning of the acts of creation, even though the days of these acts had come to an end.

"These are the generations of heaven and of earth,"[2] that is to say, this is the narrative of the establishment of heaven and earth "on the day that the Lord made heaven and earth, for none of the trees of the field had yet come into being, and the vegetation had not sprouted."[3] It is quite true that these had not been created, seeing that these were made on the third day.[4]

Now it was not without reason that Scripture introduced on the first day mention of things created on the third.

3. For it says, "The trees were not in existence and the vegetation had not yet sprouted, seeing that the Lord had not caused rain to fall on the earth. A fountain went up from the earth to irrigate the surface of the earth."[1] Since everything was and is born through the interaction of water and earth, Scripture took care to indicate that trees and vegetation were not created at the same time as the earth, seeing that rain had not yet fallen. But after the great fountain of the great primordial deep had gone up and

---

1 note 1: Gen. 2:4-6.
2 note 1: Gen. 2:3.
  note 2: Gen. 2:4.
  note 3: Gen. 2:5.
  note 4: cf Gen. 1:9-13.
3 note 1: Gen. 2:5-6.

irrigated the entire surface of the earth, then, once the waters had been gathered together on the third day, the earth gave birth to all sorts of vegetation on the very same day.

The waters over which the darkness had been spread on the first day are the same as those which issued from this fountain, covering, in a twinkling of an eye, the entire earth. This is the fountain which was opened up in the days of Noah, covering over all mountains on the earth. Now this fountain did not come up from under the earth, but from the earth, for it explicitly says "the fountain was coming up"—not *from beneath* the earth, but "*from* the earth." That these waters in the earth do not precede the earth in time is testified by the fact that the earth carries them in its womb.

So "the fountain went up from the earth," as Scripture says, "and it irrigated the surface of the entire earth." The earth then produced trees, vegetation and plants. It was not the case that God was unable to generate everything from the earth in any other way, but, because it was His will that the earth should give birth through the agency of water, He provided an initial beginning for this process, corresponding to the way in which it would be carried on until the end.

4. Having spoken about what had been omitted and left untold on the first day, Scripture reverts to the description of Adam's fashioning as follows: "And Adam was not there to work on the earth."[1] Indeed he was not in existence during all the days prior to the sixth, because it was on the sixth day that he was created.[2]

So on the sixth day "the Lord fashioned dust from the ground into Adam, and He breathed the breath of life into

4 note 1: Gen. 2:5.
note 2: Gen. 1:26-7, 31.

his nostrils, and Adam became a living being."³ Although animals, cattle and birds came into being at the same moment that they received life, in Adam's case God honored him in a variety of ways: first, because it is said that God "fashioned him with His hands and He breathed a soul into him"; He also gave him authority over Paradise and what is outside Paradise; and He wrapped him in glory* and gave him reason, thought and an awareness of the Majesty.

5. Having spoken of the honored way in which Adam was fashioned, Scripture turns to describe Paradise and Adam's introduction into it: "And the Lord planted Paradise in Eden of old, and He placed there Adam whom He had fashioned."¹

Now Eden is the land of Paradise. By "of old"* Scripture means that He planted it on the third day; it explains this with the words "the Lord caused to sprout from the earth every kind of tree that is beautiful to look upon and good to eat";² and to show that this refers to Paradise, it says, "and the Tree of Life was in the midst of Paradise, and the Tree of Knowledge of good and evil."³

6. After having spoken of Paradise and the day on which it was planted, as well as the introduction into it of Adam, and the Tree of Life and its companion, Scripture turns to describe the river which goes out from its midst, and how it is divided up outside Paradise into four sources: "A river was issuing from Eden to irrigate Paradise."¹ Notice that here too it calls the delightful land of Paradise "Eden."

Had that river not first irrigated Paradise it would not

---

4 note 3: Gen. 2:7.
5 note 1: Gen. 2:8.
   note 2: Gen. 2:9.
   note 3: Gen. 2:9.
6 note 1: Gen. 2:10.

have divided up into four sources outside it. I think it was perhaps for purposes of convenience that it was said to "irrigate," seeing that the spiritual trees of Paradise do not require any irrigation by water. But if, despite their being spiritual, they nevertheless absorbed something of those blessed and spiritual waters there, I should not object to such an opinion.

The taste of the water of the four tributaries which flow from that river is not like the taste of the head of the source. For if water varies in taste in our countries, all of which are subject to the sentence of the curse, how much more would one expect the taste in the blessed land of Eden to be different from that of the land which was laid under the curse of the Just One as a result of Adam's transgression?

Now these four rivers are as follows: the Pishon, that is, the Danube;* the Gihon, that is, the Nile; the Tigris and the Euphrates. In between these we live. Even though the regions from which these flow are known, this does not apply to the head of the source; for Paradise is situated on a great height, and the rivers are swallowed up under the surrounding sea, descending as it were down a tall water pipe;* having passed through the ground beneath the sea and reached this earth, the earth then spouts forth with one of them in the West—the Danube, or Pishon—the Gihon in the South, and the Euphrates and Tigris in the North.

7. Having spoken of Paradise and the rivers which issue from it and divide up, Scripture turns to speak of the entry of Adam into Paradise and the law which was laid down for him, as follows: "The Lord God took Adam and left him in the Paradise of Eden to till it [*or* worship Him] and keep [*or* guard] it."[1]*

---

7 note 1: Gen. 2:15.

With what did he till it, seeing that he had not agricultural implements? And how would he have been able to till it, seeing that he could not have managed it himself? And what would he have to clear from it, seeing that there were no thistles or thorns there? Again, how could he have guarded it, since he could not walk right around it? And from what was he guarding it, seeing that there was no thief trying to enter it? Now the barrier* which came into existence at the transgression of the commandment testified to the fact that no guard was required as long as the commandment was kept.

So Adam had nothing to keep there except for the law which was laid down for him. Nor was any work entrusted to him apart from preserving the commandment that he had been given. But should someone say that he had these two things to do as well as the commandment, I would not oppose him.

8. Having spoken of the introduction of Adam into Paradise and the reason God brought him there, Scripture turns to describe the commandment which was laid down for him, as follows: "And the Lord God commanded Adam, saying: 'You may indeed eat of all the trees in Paradise, but of the Tree of Knowledge of good and evil you shall not eat; for on the day you eat of it you will certainly die.' "[1]

This commandment was a light one, for God had given him the whole of Paradise and held back from him but a single tree. If one tree sufficed for someone's sustenance, and many trees were withheld from him, there would still be relief for his distress, seeing that there still existed food for his hunger. But where it is a case of God's giving him many trees when one would have been sufficient, this means that if transgression takes place, it is not as a result of any

---

8 note 1: Gen. 2:16-17.

real need, but because of contempt. So God withheld from him a single tree,* hedging it around with death, so that even if Adam were to fail to keep the law out of love for the Lawgiver, at least the fear of death that surrounded the tree would make him afraid of overstepping the law.

9. Having spoken of Adam's entry into Paradise and of the law that was laid down for him, Scripture turns to describe the names which he gave to the animals, as follows: "The Lord fashioned out of the earth all the wild animals and the birds of the sky; and He brought them to Adam to see what he would call them."[1]

They were not actually "fashioned," for the earth produced the animals, and the water the birds.[2] By saying "fashioned" Scripture wishes to indicate that all animals, reptiles, cattle and birds came into being as a result of the combining of earth and water.

It says "He brought them to Adam" in order to indicate his wisdom, and also the peaceful state which existed between the animals and Adam prior to his transgressing the commandment. For they came to him as though to a loving shepherd, passing in front of him without any fear, flock after flock according to their species and varieties. They had no fear of him, nor were they in trepidation of one another; a herd of predators passed by, followed fearlessly by a group of the animals upon which they preyed.

10. So Adam took care of the earth and became master of everything on this day, in accordance with the blessing he had received—for the word of the Creator had taken effect and his blessing had been fulfilled in actual fact. That very same day did he rule over everything; and even though Adam was quick to rebel against the Lord of all

9 note 1: Gen. 2:19.
note 2: cf Gen. 1:20.

things, God did not just give him the authority over all things that He had promised him, but in addition He gave him the right to allocate names, something that He had not promised him. Now if He had done more for him than what he had expected, how do you suppose He would have deprived him of what He had promised for any other reason than because he had sinned?

If it were a case of someone giving just a small number of names, the remembering of these would be nothing out of the ordinary, but to allocate thousands of names all in a single short moment, and to avoid any duplication between the first ones and the last, this is something which surpasses human ability. For someone to specify a multitude of names for a multitude of species—reptiles, wild animals, domestic cattle and birds—is quite possible, but to avoid ever calling one species by the name of another is something that belongs to God—or to a human being to whom this ability has been given by God. If God gave Adam authority, made him share in the act of creation, wrapped him in glory, and gave him the Garden, what else should He have done for him so that he might keep the commandment, but did not do?

11. After speaking about the fashioning of the animals and of the names they received, Scripture turns to describe Adam's sleep and the rib which was removed from him, and how woman [*or* a wife] was established, in the following words: "For Adam there was to be found no helper who resembled himself."[1] Scripture calls Eve "helper," seeing that, even if Adam had helpers among the animals and cattle, nevertheless a helper of his own kind would be useful to him. For Eve looked after things inside, caring for the sheep, oxen, herds, and flocks in the field; she also assisted him with the buildings and the sheepfolds, and

11 note 1: Gen. 2:20.

with the crafts that he invented. For even though the animals were subject to him, they were unable to assist him in these sorts of things. For that reason God made him a helper who would take care of everything along with him. And indeed she did assist him in all sorts of ways.

12. "The Lord cast a stillness on Adam and he slept; He took one of his ribs and closed up the flesh in its place. And the Lord made the rib that He had taken from Adam into a woman, and He brought her to Adam."[1] Now the man, who was wakeful,* anointed with radiance, and as yet ignorant of what sleep was, fell naked on the ground and slept. It is quite likely that he saw in his dream what was being done to him in waking life.

Once the rib had been extracted in the twinkling of an eye, and God had closed up the flesh in the flicker of an eyelid, and the bare rib had been fashioned with all kinds of adornments and embellishments, God then took her and brought her to Adam who was both one and two: he was one because he was Adam, he was two because he was created male and female.

13. Having spoken of the stillness, the extracted rib and the woman fashioned out of it who had been brought to him, Scripture describes how Adam said, "This time it is bone from my bone and flesh from my flesh; let her be called woman, for she is taken from man."[1] "This time" refers to the fact that she came after the animals and did not resemble them. For they came into being from the earth, whereas she "is bone from my bones and flesh from my flesh." He may have said this of her as though in

12 note 1: Gen. 2:21-22.
13 note 1: Gen. 2:23

prophecy, or he knew it was the case from the visionary dream he had seen, as we suggested above.

Seeing that all species of animals had received from him a name on that very day, Adam did not call the rib that had been fashioned by her personal name "Eve," but called her instead "woman," the generic name applying to her entire kind.

He said "a man shall leave his father and his mother and attach himself to his wife"[2] so that they might be united and the two of them become one, without division, as they were originally.

14.   Following this it says, "The two of them were naked, but they were not ashamed."[1] It was not because they were ignorant of what shame was that they were not ashamed; for had they been infants,* as the pagans say, Scripture would not have said that "they were naked but were not ashamed," nor would it have spoken of "Adam and his wife" had they not been adults. The names which Adam gave should convince us of his wisdom, and the fact that it says that "he was to work it and guard it" is to indicate his strength. Likewise, the law laid down for them is meant to testify to their adulthood—and the transgression of the law to testify to their arrogance.

It was because of the glory in which they were wrapped that they were not ashamed. Once this had been taken away from them, after the transgression of the commandment, they were ashamed because they had been stripped of it, and the two of them rushed to the leaves in order to cover not so much their bodies as their shameful members.

15.   Having spoken of their naked state—which, because

---

13 note 2: Gen. 2:24.
14 note 1: Gen. 2:25.

it was adorned with a heavenly raiment, was not shameful
—Scripture turns to write about the astuteness of the
serpent, as follows: "And the serpent was more astute than
all the other wild animals that the Lord had made."[1] Now
even though it was astute, it was only more astute than the
dumb animals which are under the control of mankind: it
had not yet, just by reason of its having surpassed the level
of animals in its astuteness, been raised to the level of
mankind. That irrational creature was only more astute
than the cattle; that mindless serpent was only more crafty
than other animals. For it is clear that the serpent did
not have a human mind, seeing that it did not possess
human wisdom; whereas Adam, who surpassed the serpent
in the way he was fashioned, by having a soul and an
intellect, by his glory and by his location, clearly also in-
finitely surpassed the serpent in astuteness. For Adam,
who had been set in authority and control over animals,
was wiser than all the animals, and he who gave names to
them all was certainly more astute than them all. For just
as Israel could not look upon the face of Moses,[2] neither
were the animals able to look upon the radiance of Adam
and Eve: at the time when they received names from him
they passed in front of Adam with their eyes down, since
their eyes were incapable of taking in his glory. So even
though the serpent was more astute than the other animals,
compared to Adam and Eve, who had authority over
animals, it was foolish.

16. Having spoken of the serpent's astuteness, it turns to
describe how the deceitful one came to Eve, as follows:
"And the serpent said to the woman, 'Did God really tell
you not to eat of any of the trees of Paradise?' "[1] On the

---

15 note 1: Gen. 3:1.
　　 note 2: Exod. 34:33-35 (Moses' descent from Mt Sinai).
16 note 1: Gen. 3:1.

matter of the serpent's words: either Adam knew the
serpent's own language, or Satan spoke through it*; or
the serpent asked the question mentally, and speech was
granted it, or Satan asked God that speech should temporarily be granted to the serpent.

Now the tempter's words would not have caused the
tempted pair to sin had not their greed abetted the tempter.
And even if the tempter had not come, the Tree with all
its beauty would have caused them a struggle with their
greed. In other words, they used the serpent's counsel as
an excuse, for it was their own greed, which conformed
with the serpent's counsel and went beyond it, that brought
harm upon them.

17. For it says, "The woman saw that the Tree was
good to eat, and was delightful to the eyes; and the Tree
was enticing to look upon, and so she took some of its
fruit and ate."[1] Now if she was overcome by the Tree's
beauty and by desire for its fruit, she was not overcome
by the counsel that had entered her ear, seeing that she
was defeated by the greed which issued from within herself.

Seeing that a commandment had been laid down for the
tempted pair, it was appropriate that the tempter should
come momentarily. Now because God had given to Adam
everything inside and outside Paradise through Grace,
requiring nothing in return, either for his creation, or for
the glory in which He had clothed him, nevertheless out
of Justice He held back one tree from him to whom He
had given, in Grace, everything in Paradise and on earth, in
the air and in the seas. For when God created Adam, He
did not make him mortal, nor did He fashion him as
immortal; this was so that Adam himself, either through
keeping the commandment, or by transgressing it, might

17 note 1: Gen. 3:6.

acquire from this one of the trees whichever outcome he wanted.

God had created the Tree of Life and hidden it from Adam and Eve, first, so that it should not, with its beauty, stir up conflict with them and so double their struggle, and also because it was inappropriate that they should be observant of the commandment of Him who cannot be seen for the sake of a reward that was there before their eyes.

Even though God had given them everything else out of Grace, He wished to confer on them, out of Justice, the immortal life which is granted through eating of the Tree of Life. He therefore laid down this commandment. Not that it was a large commandment, commensurate with the superlative reward that was in preparation for them; no, He only withheld from them a single tree, just so that they might be subject to a commandment. But He gave them the whole of Paradise, so that they would not feel any compulsion to transgress the law.

18. Because a tempter was required, as I mentioned, Satan was not allowed to have one of the Watchers, or one of the Seraphim or Cherubim, sent to Adam for this purpose; nor was Satan allowed to come to Adam in the Garden in human appearance, or in the divine appearance in which he came to our Lord on the mountain.[1] Nor did any of the huge and renowned animals, such as Behemoth or Leviathan, come; nor did any of the other animals, or any of the ritually clean cattle, lest some excuse might be found by [or for] the transgressors of the commandment. Instead, a mere serpent was allowed to come to them, which, even if it was astute, was nevertheless utterly despised and despicable.

Moreover, when the serpent came, it did not do so performing any signs, or even fashioning some false appari-

18 note 1: Matt. 4:1-11 and parallels.

tion; no, it came just by itself in its mean state, with down-cast eyes seeing that it was unable to look upon the radiance of her who was being tempted by this creature. Out of fear it did not go to Adam, but went instead to Eve, in order quickly to get her to eat of the Tree from which she had been told not to eat. And this was when she had not yet tasted of the thousands and ten thousands of other trees that had been granted her. And the reason for her not having tasted them was not because she was fasting; rather, hunger had not yet gained any hold over her, for she had only just been created at that very time.

The entire reason the serpent was not prevented from coming hastily was because the serpent's very haste worked against the serpent. For it was the moment that Eve had been created, and she did not yet know what hunger was; and up to now she had not been tormented by any struggle over the Tree's beauty. So, because she was not hungry and was not struggling with the Tree, the serpent was not prevented from becoming a tempter.

If she had vanquished it in a momentary fight, in a struggle lasting but a short time, the serpent—and he who was in the serpent—would still have received the punishment which in the event they received, while she and her husband would have eaten of the Tree of Life and lived forever; with the promised life that they would have acquired through Justice, they would also have had, through Justice, everything that previously they had been given through Grace.

So the tempter made haste to come, and was not prevented. This was so that they might realize that he was the tempter, by the fact that the tempter came at the same time as the commandment, and in this way they would be wary of his deceitfulness. He who was unable to provide himself with even a small reputation came along and gave them momentous counsel.

19. Satan, who was in the serpent, spoke through the serpent to the woman: "Did God really say that you should not eat of any of the trees of Paradise?"[1] It is right that we should realize that, had they been commanded not to eat of any of the trees, as the serpent said, it would have been a big commandment. Whereas in fact they were commanded exactly the opposite, as it were, no commandment at all seeing that it was so small and had been given only temporarily, until the tempter had gone away from them.

Now Eve replied, saying to the serpent, "From the fruits of the trees in Paradise we may eat, but from the fruits of the Tree in the middle of Paradise He told us not to eat and not to approach it, lest we die."[2] The serpent, and he who was in the serpent, having heard that all the trees of Paradise had been provided for fruit, and only one had been withheld from them, supposed themselves to be wrapped in shame, seeing that there was no opportunity for counseling disobedience.

20. Accordingly, the tempter observed the commandment of God the giver of commandments, how not only had they been forbidden to eat of it, but they were not to approach it at all; and he realized that God had forewarned them away from seeing the Tree, lest they be captivated by its beauty. So, luring Eve to look at it, he said, "It is not the case that you will die, for God knows that the day you eat of these fruits your eyes will be opened, and you will become like God, knowing good and evil."[1] Now Eve omitted to look carefully at the serpent's words, at how the tempter had said exactly the opposite of what had been uttered by God; and she failed to answer him back and say, "How can my eyes be opened, seeing

19 note 1: Gen. 3:1.
   note 2: Gen. 3:2-3.
20 note 1: Gen. 3:4-5.

that they are not closed?" and "How will I know the
difference between good and evil by eating the fruit, seeing
that I already know this before eating it?" But she neglected
everything that she should have said in opposition to the
serpent, and, just as the serpent had desired, she raised her
eyes from the serpent in front of her and gazed at the Tree
she had been commanded not to approach. Now the serpent
kept quiet, for it already perceived her guilt. For it was
not so much the counsel that had entered her ear that lured
her on to eat of the Tree, but rather her gaze, which she
had focused on the Tree, enticed her to pluck and eat
some of its fruit.

She could very well have said to the serpent, "If I cannot see, how is it that I see everything that is to be seen?
And if I do not know the difference between good and
evil, how could I discern whether your counsel is good or
evil? How would I know that divinity was good and the
opening of the eyes an excellent thing, and whence would
I recognize that death is evil? But all this is available to
me; so why have you come to me? Your coming to us
bears witness that we possess these very things; for with
the sight that I have, and with the ability to distinguish
what is good from what is evil that I possess, I will test
your counsel. If I already have the things which you have
promised, where is all this cunning of yours which has
failed to hide your deception?"

She did not say these things whereby she might have defeated the serpent, but instead she fixed her gaze on the
Tree, thereby hastening her own defeat. Thus, following
her desire and enticed by the divinity which the serpent
had promised her, she ate furtively, away from her husband. Only subsequently did she give it to her husband,
and he ate with her. Because she had believed the serpent,
she ate first, imagining that she would return clothed in
divinity to her husband whom she had left as a woman.
She hastily ate before her husband so that she might become

head over her head, and that she might be giving orders to him from whom she received orders, seeing that she had become senior in divinity to Adam to whom she was junior in humanity.

21. When she had eaten, she neither grew nor shrank; nor did she acquire enlightenment. For she did not receive the divinity she had been looking to, nor did she find the enlightenment that brings one to Paradise. She took the fruit to her husband and, with many entreaties, got him to eat it—though it is not written that she entreated him.[1]

Having once eaten, Eve did not die as God had said, nor did she find divinity, as the serpent had said. For had she been exposed, Adam would have been afraid and would not have eaten, in which case, even though he would not have been guilty in that he did not eat, yet he would not have been victorious either, seeing that he would not have been tempted. It would have been the exposing of his wife that would have restrained him from eating rather than love for, or fear of, Him who gave the commandment. It was so that Adam might for a moment be tempted by Eve's blandishments—just as she had been by the counsel of the serpent—that she had approached and eaten, but had not been exposed.

22. Once Eve had enticed Adam and gotten him to eat, Scripture says that "the eyes of the two of them were opened and they knew that they were naked."[1] So their eyes were opened, not that they might become like God, as the serpent had said, but that they might see their own exposure, just as the enemy had hoped. For their eyes had thus been both open and closed: open, in that they could

21 note 1: cf Gen. 3:6.
22 note 1: Gen. 3:7.

see everything; but closed, in that they did not see either the Tree of Life or their own exposure.

The enemy was envious* for this reason too, because they surpassed everything on earth in possessing glory and reason, and eternal life which is provided by the Tree of Life was promised to them alone. Thus the enemy was envious of Adam and Eve both for what they had and for what they were to receive; accordingly, he plotted against them and in the course of a momentary struggle he took from them what they should not have lost even if it meant a great struggle.

23. For had the serpent been rejected, along with the sin, they would have eaten of the Tree of Life, and the Tree of Knowledge would not have been withheld from them any longer; from the one they would have acquired infallible knowledge, and from the other they would have received immortal life. They would have acquired divinity* in humanity; and had they thus acquired infallible knowledge and immortal life they would have done so in this body.

Thus by what it promised, the serpent annulled what they were to have had: it made them think that they would receive this by transgressing the commandment, thus effecting that they would not receive it as a result of keeping the commandment. It withheld divinity from them by means of the divinity which it promised them, and it brought about that those, to whom it had promised enlightenment from the Tree of Knowledge, should not have their eyes illumined by the Tree of Life, as promised.

Now had they been willing to repent after transgressing the commandment, even though they would not have received what they had possessed prior to their transgression, nevertheless they would have escaped from the curses pronounced over the earth and over themselves. For the whole reason for God's delay in coming down to them was in case they might rebuke one another and so, when the Judge did come to them, they might ask for mercy. The serpent's arrival was not delayed, so that their temptation at the beautiful sight of the Tree might not be too great. The Judge, on the other hand, did delay in coming to them, in order to give them an opportunity to prepare a plea. However, the haste on the part of the tempter did not help them, even though this haste was designed to help them; nor did they profit from the Judge's delay, even though His delay, too, was intended for that very purpose.

24. "And they heard the sound [*or* voice] of the Lord as He walked in Paradise at the turn of the day; and they hid themselves from the Lord's presence among the trees in Paradise."[1]

It was not just by the patience that He showed toward them that He wanted to help them, but He also wanted the sound of His footsteps to assist them; for He caused His silent footsteps to make a noise so that, at the noise, they might prepare to make supplication before Him who issued the sound. When, however, they failed to appear before Him with supplication, either as a result of His delay or because of the sound that had been sent forth in advance of Him, God then went on to employ the sound of His lips, just as He had used the sound of His footsteps, saying "Where are you, Adam?"[2] But instead of confessing his wrong and asking mercy before sentence was pronounced over him, Adam said, "I heard the sound of You in Paradise and I was afraid, for I saw that I was naked and so I hid myself."[3]

The sound of feet which went before the God who was about to be revealed to Adam and Eve in punishment pre-

---

24 note 1: Gen. 3:8.
   note 2: Gen. 3:9.
   note 3: Gen. 3:10.

figured the voice of John* who was to come before the
Son, holding a winnowing fan in his hands as he cleans
his threshing floors, about to burn the chaff in fire and
clean the wheat in order to bring it into his storehouses.[4]

25. "I heard the sound of You and I hid myself."[1] When
had you heard the sound of Him as you do now? For you
did not hear His sound when He fashioned you and brought
you into Paradise, nor when He cast a stillness upon you
and extracted your rib, constructing and bringing to you
a wife. If it is only just recently that you have heard the
sound of Him, you should realize even now that this sound
of footsteps was made in order that your lips might make
supplication. Speak to Him before He questions you about
the coming of the serpent and about your and Eve's transgression, in case the confession of your lips might absolve
you of the sin of eating the fruit which your fingers plucked.

But they failed to confess anything about what they
had done; instead, they told the Omniscient what had
happened to them.

26. "Where are you, Adam? In the state of divinity
which the serpent promised you? Or subject to death which
I pronounced over you, should you look to the fruits?

Now suppose, Adam, that instead of the utterly despicable serpent there had come to you an angel, or another
divine being, would it have been right for you to despise
the command of Him who gave you all these things and
instead to listen to the counsel of one who had not yet in
actual fact performed anything good for you? Would you
consider as evil Him who fashioned you out of nothing
and made you a second god over creation, instead holding
to be good one who had merely with words promised you

24 note 4: cf Matt. 3:12.
25 note 1: Gen. 3:10.

some advantage? And if it would not be right for you to be deceived by the counsel of some other god, were he to come to you with a show of force, how much more so when it is a serpent that has come to you, without any mighty acts or miracles, but with only the bare words which it addressed to you? You have held your God to be false and your deceiver to be true; you have broken faith with your Benefactor who put you in authority over everything, and you have believed that deceiver who has cunningly managed to take away your authority completely."

Had the serpent been prevented from coming to tempt Adam, the people who today complain about its having come would be complaining about its having been prevented from coming; for they would be saying that the serpent—who in fact came so that Adam might acquire eternal life by means of a short-lived temptation—had been prevented from doing so out of envy. And those who now say that Adam would never have gone astray if the serpent had not come would instead be saying that had the serpent come, Adam would not have gone astray. For, just as they imagine that they are doing well by saying, "Had the serpent not come, Adam and Eve would not have gone astray," all the more so would they imagine that they did well by saying, "Had the serpent come, it would not have led Adam and Eve astray." Indeed, who would ever have believed it, had it not actually happened, that Adam should have listened to a serpent or Eve been won over by a reptile!

27. "I heard the sound of You, and I was afraid and hid myself."[1] Because Adam omitted what was requisite and instead said something that was not required—for instead of confessing what he had done, which would have benefited him, he related what had happened to him,

---

27 note 1: Gen. 3:10.

which did not benefit him—God said to him, "Who showed you that you are naked? You have eaten of the Tree from which I commanded you not to eat.[2] You have seen your own nakedness with the help of the vision which the Tree bestowed upon you—the same that had promised you a glorious vision of divinity."

Once again Adam failed to confess his fault, laying the blame on the woman who was like him: "The woman with whom you provided me gave me of the Tree and I ate.[3] I myself did not approach the Tree, nor was it my hand which presumed to stretch out for the fruit." This is why the Apostle too says, "Adam himself did not sin, but Eve transgressed the commandment."[4]

But if He gave you a wife, Adam, He gave her as a helper and not as a harmer, as someone who receives instructions, rather than as one who gives orders.

28. When Adam was unwilling to confess his fault, God went down to Eve with a question, saying to her, "What is this that you have done?"[1] Eve, too, instead of making supplication with tears and taking the fault upon herself in the hope that pardon might come upon herself and her husband, answered back, not saying, "The serpent counseled me" or "enticed me," but simply, "The serpent deceived me and I ate."[2]

29. When the two of them had been questioned and found to be lacking in contrition or valid excuse, God descended to the serpent, not with a question, but with a punishment. For where there was a possibility of repentance He made use of questions, but with a creature that is

---

27 note 2: Gen. 3:11.
    note 3: Gen. 3:12.
    note 4: 1 Tim. 2:14.
28 note 1: Gen. 3:13.
    note 2: Gen. 3:13.

alien to repentance He employed a sentence of judgment.
And you should realize that the serpent cannot repent
from the fact that, when God said to it, "Because you have
done this you are more cursed than all cattle,"[1] it did not
say "I did not do it" because it was afraid to lie, nor did
it say "I did it," because it was alien to repentance.

"You are more cursed than all cattle because you deceived those who have authority over all cattle; and instead
of being more astute than all other animals you shall be
more cursed than all other animals, and you shall go about
on your belly because you brought pangs upon womankind.
And you shall eat dust all the days of your life[2] because
you deprived Adam and Eve of the food of the Tree of
Life. And I will place enmity between you and the woman,
and between your seed and her seed[3] because by your
fraudulent show of love you deceived and subjected both
her and her children to death."

He then indicates the nature of the enmity which was
placed between the serpent and the woman, between its
seed and hers, saying, "It shall tread upon your head—
which wanted to escape from subjugation to her seed—and
you will strike it, not in its organ of hearing, but in its
heel."[4]

30. Now even though the sentence imposed on the serpent
was justly decreed—for punishment reverts to where the
crime originated—nevertheless the full reason God began
with this despicable creature was so that Adam and Eve
might become afraid and repent while Justice was appeasing
its anger on the serpent: then there would be an opportunity for Grace to hold them back from Justice's curses.

---

29 note 1: Gen. 3:14.
   note 2: Gen. 3:14.
   note 3: Gen. 3:15.
   note 4: Gen. 3:15.

When the serpent had been cursed, however, and Adam
and Eve still did not ask forgiveness, God then came with
punishment. He came to Eve, since it was by her hand
that the sin had been handed over to Adam. Thus he
decreed as follows against Eve: "I will greatly multiply
your pains and your conceptions, and you shall give birth
to children with pangs."[1]

Even though she would have given birth to children
anyway—seeing that she had received the blessing of
childbirth along with all creatures—nevertheless she would
not have given birth to many children, because those whom
she bore would have remained immortal. And she would
have been spared the pangs of birthgiving, the anguish of
their upbringing and the lamentations at their deaths.

"And you shall turn to your husband"—to be counseled,
and not to counsel—"and he shall have authority over
you"[2]—since you imagined that by eating the fruit you
would from then onward have authority over him.

31.   After He had decreed concerning Eve and repentance
failed to spring up in Adam, He then turned to him as
well in punishment, saying, "Because you listened to the
voice of your wife and were wheedled into eating of the
Tree from which I told you not to eat, cursed is the earth
because of you."[1]

Although it was the earth, which had not done wrong,
which was smitten instead of Adam, who had done wrong,
nevertheless it was Adam, who is subject to suffering, whom
He caused to suffer by means of the curse on the earth,
which is not subject to suffering; for it was because of the
earth's being cursed that Adam, who had not been directly
cursed, was cursed. Thus he did not escape punishment at

---

30 note 1: Gen. 3:16.
    note 2: Gen. 3:16.
31 note 1: cf Gen. 3:17.

the curse which the earth received, for God decreed concerning him too, as follows: "With pains shall you eat of it all the days of your life—that is, after breaking the commandment, though you would have eaten of it without any pains had the commandment been kept. Thorns and thistles will it bring forth after the sin, things which it would not have brought forth had there been no sin. You shall eat herbage of the field, because through your wife's slight enticement you have rejected Paradise's delectable fruits. With the sweat of your face will you eat bread, because it did not please you to enjoy yourself without any toil in the delights of the Garden. All this will be your portion until you return to the earth whence you were taken, seeing that you despised the commandment which, at the very present moment, might have given you eternal life, by means of the fruit of the Tree of Life which you would have been permitted to eat. Since you originate from dust and you forgot yourself, you shall return to your dust and your true being shall be recognized through your low estate."[2]

32. Even Satan, who was created within these six days along with the womb to which he belonged, was fair until the sixth day, just as Adam and Eve were fair up to the time they transgressed the commandment. Now Satan, who had become Satan in secret on this day, was also secretly sentenced and condemned the same day; for God did not wish to make known his judgment in the presence of the pair who were not aware of his having tempted them—the woman said "It was the serpent," and not Satan, "who led me astray." So Satan was judged secretly, and in him all his hosts were condemned. For since the sin was so great, and any one of them alone would have been too insignificant for the punishment—just as birth pangs were decreed

31 note 2: cf Gen. 3:17-19, expanded.

for Eve along with her daughters, and pains and death for
Adam and his children, and for the serpent it was decreed
that it and all its seed should be trampled—so it was
decreed against Satan who was in the serpent that he
should go to the fire along with all his hosts. For in the
New Testament our Lord revealed what had been hidden
in the old, when he said, "Concerning the judgment of the
ruler of this world, he is judged," that is, he is condemned.[1]

33.   Having spoken of the punishment which the tempter
and those tempted received, Scripture describes how "the
Lord made garments of skin* for Adam and Eve, and
clothed them."[1] Whether these garments were from the
skins of animals, or whether they were specially created,
like the thorn bushes and thistles which were created after
the other works of creation had been completed, seeing
that it is said that "the Lord made . . . and clothed them,"
it seems likely that when their hands were laid upon their
leaves they found themselves clothed with garments made
of skin. Or were, perhaps, some animals killed before
them, so that they could nourish themselves with their
flesh, cover up their nakedness with their skins, and in
their deaths see the death of their own bodies?

34.   Having finished this it says, "Behold, Adam has become like one of us, knowing good and evil."[1] By saying
that "he has become like one of us," Scripture also revealed
symbolically something about the Trinity.* But at the same
time God was actually addressing Adam ironically, seeing
that Adam had been told, "you will become like God,
knowing good and evil."

However, although Adam and Eve became aware of

32 note 1: John 16:11.
33 note 1: Gen. 3:21.
34 note 1: Gen. 3:22.

both these things from eating the fruit, prior to the fruit they were in practice only aware of the good, hearing about evil by report, but after eating it there was a change, so that they only heard by report of the good, whereas they tasted evil in practice. For the glory in which they had been wrapped left them, and the pains which had previously been kept away from them now dominated them.

35. "And now, lest he stretch out his hand and take from the fruit of the Tree of Life as well, and eat it and live for ever . . ."[1] For if he had the audacity to eat of the Tree of which he was commanded not to eat, how much the more would he make a dash for the Tree concerning which he had received no commandment? But because it had been decreed against them that they should exist in toil and sweat, in pains and pangs, God, who when they were still free from the curse and clothed in glory was prepared to give them immortal life, now that they were clothed in the curse, kept them back from eating of the Tree of Life, lest by eating of it and living forever, they would have to remain in a life of pain for eternity.

God's intention, then, was that this life-giving gift, which they would have received from the Tree of Life, might not be turned to misery and actually harm them even more than what they had acquired through the Tree of Knowledge. For from the Tree of Knowledge they had acquired temporal pains, whereas the Tree of Life would have made those pains eternal. From the Tree of Knowledge they had acquired death which would release them from the bonds of their pains, whereas the Tree of Life would have made them entombed all their lives, leaving them forever tortured by their pains. So it was that God kept them back from the Tree of Life, for it was not appropriate, either

---

35 note 1: Gen. 3:22.

that a life of delight should be provided in the land of curses, or that eternal life should be found in the transient world.

Had they eaten, however, one of two things would have happened: either the sentence of death would have been proved false, or the life-giving characteristic of the Tree of Life would have been proved not to be genuine. In order, therefore, that the sentence of death might not be annulled, and the life-giving characteristic of the Tree might not be proved false, God kept Adam at a distance from it, lest he suffer loss from the Tree of Life as well, just as he had already been harmed by the Tree of Knowledge.

God now sends him "to work the earth from which he had been taken,"[2] so that he who had been harmed by the ease in the Garden might be benefited by toil on the earth.

36. At his departure from Paradise it says that God "caused a cherub and a sharp revolving sword to go round, to the east of the Garden of Eden, to protect the way to the Tree of Life."[1] The barrier was thus a living one, which of its own accord went around guarding the way to the Tree of Life from anyone who audaciously wanted to pluck its fruit; for it would kill with its sharp sword any mortal who came to steal for himself immortal life.

---

35 note 2: Gen. 3:23.
36 note 1: Gen. 3:24.

Notes to Section II of the Commentary on Genesis

(Marked with asterisks in the text)

II.1 *Scripture*: the subject of the verb in this frequently occurring phrase is mostly left unexpressed.
already spoken of: in Genesis 1. St Ephrem sees Gen. 1 as giving the chronological framework for creation, while Gen. 2-3 go back and expand on certain details.

II.4 *wrapped him in glory*: for Adam's original "Robe of Glory" see the Introduction.

II.5 *of old*: the Hebrew can be understood as "from the East" or "of old"; see the Introduction.

II.6 *Pishon . . . Danube*: various identifications of the river Pishon are found in early Jewish and Christian writers (the Ganges and the Don are among the other candidates). The identification of the Gihon as the Nile is standard.
water pipe: Ephrem uses the Greek word *sōlēn*. It is interesting that in pagan writers this imagery is sometimes used to denote the descent of the soul into the body. Ephrem clearly wants to emphasize that Paradise and earth belong to two different orders of being (on this point, see also the Introduction).

II.7 *till (worship) . . . keep (guard)*: The Syriac (and Hebrew) text of Genesis 2:15 is ambiguous. In the following paragraph Ephrem seeks to show that "keep" makes much better exegetical sense, with the commandment as the object. This is in line with the rendering of the verse in the Palestinian Targum tradition: "The Lord God took Adam and caused him to dwell in the Garden of Eden, to labor with the Law and to keep His commandment." On this interpretation the beginning of Genesis 2:16 will have been under-

stood in the sense "Now the Lord God *had* commanded . . ."
barrier (syāgā): for this term see the Introduction.

II.8   *a single tree*: throughout his exegesis of Genesis 2-3 Ephrem
        is at pains to point out that Adam and Eve had absolutely
        no excuse for their transgression of God's commandment,
        and that they then failed to take advantage of His patience
        and efforts to get them to repent of their sin.

II.12   *wakeful*: the word can also be translated "a Watcher," a
        term for angelic beings which Ephrem derives from the book
        of Daniel (cf Hymn VI.23). For the ideal of the angelic
        life, see the Introduction.

II.14   *infants*: though Ephrem attributes this view to "pagans"
        (literally "those outside"; perhaps some heretical Christian
        group is really meant), it is also found in several early
        Christian writers such as Theophilius of Antioch (*To Auto-
        lycus* II.25); indeed Ephrem himself speaks of their
        shabrūthā, "childlike state," in the Paradise Hymns (VII.6,
        XV.12.14), but, as Beck points out in his commentary
        (pp. 67-8), the term there is not to be understood literally
        but rather it must have the metaphorical sense of "inex-
        perience." Compare Murray, *Symbols of Church and King-
        dom*, pp. 304-6.

II.16   *Satan spoke through it*: for Satan as the hidden instigator
        see Wisdom of Solomon 2:24.

II.22   *The enemy was envious*: according to a widespread Jewish
        tradition Satan's fall came about through envy at the glorious
        state in which Adam had originally been created.

II.23   *They would have acquired divinity*: see Introduction.

II.24   *prefigured the voice of John*: this is one of the rare passages
        in the Commentary on Genesis where specific reference is
        made to a New Testament theme.

II.33   *garments of skin*: the phrase gave rise to a great deal of
        speculation, and a number of very different explanations
        were put forward, notably:

        1. The Hebrew word was read as *'wr,* "light," instead of
           'wr, "skin," and the verse was taken to refer to the pre-
           Fall state (i.e. "God had made"). This is found in some
           early Jewish texts and it is the source of the phrases
           "robe of light/glory," so common in Syriac writers (see
           Introduction). A variant on this interpretation, found
           in the Jewish Targums, takes the "garments of glory"

to refer to Adam's priestly garments which he took from Paradise.

2. The garments were indeed of animal skin (a possibility which Ephrem envisages), but the implication that an animal had previously been killed led some to suppose that:

3. the "skin" was in fact the bark from trees. This view was adopted by many later Syriac writers, basing themselves on Theodore of Mopsuestia.

4. The "garments of skin" were taken by some (notably Origen) to refer to the human body, implying that the pre-Fall body had been of a different order.

II.34 *Trinity*: Ephrem, in common with most of the Fathers, understands passages where God speaks in the first person plural (such as Gen. 3:22) as pointing to the Trinity.

4.
BIBLIOGRAPHICAL NOTE

The translation is made from Dom Edmund Beck's edition of the Syriac text in *Corpus Scriptorum Christianorum Orientalium,* volume 174 (= Scriptores Syri, volume 78; Louvain, 1957). This edition replaces the earlier partial editions by Assemani (Hymns I-XII) and Overbeck (Hymns XII-XV). There are three modern translations of the complete cycle: in German (by Beck in CSCO 175 = Scr. Syri 79), in Latin (by Beck in his *Ephraems Hymnen über das Paradies,* on which see below), and in French (by R. Lavenant, with introduction and notes by F. Graffin, in *Sources chrétiennes* 137, 1968). All these I have consulted with profit, even though my understanding of some obscure passages may differ from theirs.

Dom E. Beck has provided a valuable running commentary, accompanied by a Latin translation, in *Ephraems Hymnen über das Paradies (Studia Anselmiana* 26, 1951). Much in the way of commentary that is relevant to the cycle will also be found in T. Kronholm's *Motifs from Genesis 1-11 in the Genuine Hymns of Ephrem the Syrian* (Lund, 1978).

On specific aspects or points of detail in the Hymns on Paradise the following are available:

E. Beck, "Eine christliche Parallele zu den Paradiesesjungfrauen des Korans?" *Orientalia Christiana Periodica* 14 (1948), pp. 398-405. (On VII.18).

_____, "Les Houris du Coran et Ephrem le Syrien," *Mélanges de l'Institut dominicain d'Etudes orientales du Caire* 6 (1961), pp. 405-8. (On VII.18).

_____, "Ephräms Hymnus de Paradiso XV.1-8," *Oriens Christianus* 62 (1978), pp. 24-35.

J. Daniélou, "Terre et Paradis chez les Pères de l'Eglise," *Eranos-Jahrbuch* 1953 (vol. 22, Zurich, 1954), pp. 433-72.

_____, "Catéchèse pascale et retour au Paradis," *La Maison-Dieu* 45 (1956), pp. 99-119.

T. Kronholm, "The Trees of Paradise in the Hymns of Ephrem Syrus," *Annual of the Swedish Theological Institute* 12 (1978), pp. 48-56.

R. Murray, "The Lance which re-opened Paradise," *Orientalia Christiana Periodica* 39 (1973), pp. 224-34, 401.

I. Ortiz de Urbina, "Le Paradis eschatologique d'après Saint Ephrem," *Orientalia Christiana Periodica* 21 (1955), pp. 467-72.

N. Sed, "Les hymnes sur le Paradis de Saint Ephrem et les traditions juives," *Le Muséon* 81 (1968), pp. 455-501.

J. Teixidor, "Le thème de la descente aux enfers chez saint Ephrem," *L'Orient Syrien* 6 (1961), pp. 25-40.

P. Yousif, "Le croix de Jésus et le Paradis d'Éden," *Parole d'Orient* 6/7 (1975/6), pp. 29-48.

For more general introductions to St Ephrem's thought the following may be mentioned:

T. Bou Mansour, *La pensée symbolique de Saint Ephrem Le Syrien* (Kaslik, 1988).

S. P. Brock, "The poet as theologian," *Sobornost* VII:4 (1977), pp. 243-50.

_____, *The Harp of the Spirit*: *Eighteen Poems of St Ephrem* (2nd edition, London, 1983).

_____, *The Luminous Eye*: *the Spiritual World Vision of St Ephrem* (Rome, 1985; Kalamazoo, 1990).

A. de Halleux, "Saint Ephrem le Syrien," *Revue théologique de Louvain* 14 (1983), pp. 328-55.

_____, "Mar Ephrem, théologien," *Parole de l'Orient* 4 (1973) pp. 35-54.

_____, "Ephräm der Syrer," in M. Greschat (ed.), *Gestalten der Kirchengeschichte*, I (Stuttgart, 1984), pp. 284-301.

N. El-Khoury, *Die Interpretation der Welt bei Ephraem dem Syrer* (Mainz, 1976).

L. Leloir, "L'actualité du message d'Ephrem," *Parole de l'Orient* 4 (1973) pp. 55-72.

J. Martikainen, "Ephraem der Syrer," in H. Fries and G. Kretschmar (eds.), *Klassiker der Theologie*, I (Munich, 1981), pp. 62-75.

R. Murray, *Symbols of Church and Kingdom* (Cambridge, 1975).

_____, "The theory of symbolism in St Ephrem's theology,"
Parole de l'Orient 6/7 (1975/6), pp. 1-20. (There is a French
translation of this important article in *Lettre de Ligugé* 203
(1980), pp. 7-25).

P. Yousif, *L'Eucharistie chez Saint Ephrem de Nisibe (Orientalia
Christiana Analecta* 224, 1984).

Several reliable encyclopedia articles are available: E. Beck in
Dictionnaire de Spiritualité and *Reallexikon für Antike und Chris-
tentum,* L. Leloir in *Dictionnaire d'Histoire et de Géographie
Ecclésiastique,* and R. Murray in *Catholic Dictionary of Theology*
and *Theologische Realenzyklopädie.* A fairly detailed introduction
to St Ephrem's hymns, their syllabic patterns and their transmission,
entitled "Materials for the study of the writings of St Ephrem," is
to appear in the series *Aufstieg und Niedergang der römischen
Welt.*

A convenient listing of the Greek texts attributed to Ephrem will
be found in M. Geerard, *Clavis Patrum Graecorum* II (Turnhout,
1974), pp. 366-468; the best introduction to this material is provided by D. Hemmerdinger-Iliadou in *Dictionnaire de Spiritualité*
IV, col. 800-819, supplemented by her article in *Epetēris Hetaireias
Byzantinōn Spoudōn* 42 (1975/6), pp. 320-73.

A bibliography of works on St Ephrem is provided in *Parole de
l'Orient* 4 (1973) and (for 1971-85) *Parole de l'Orient* 10 (1983)
and 14 (1987).

St Ephrem's works

The earliest printed editions in the sixteenth and seventeenth
centuries were of works in Latin and Greek attributed to St Ephrem,
and it was not until the eighteenth century, with the massive six-
volume Roman edition (1732-46), edited by P. Benedictus (Mo-
barak) and S. E. Assemani, that any of the Syriac originals became
available to the European world. The nineteenth century witnessed
further editions, by J. J. Overbeck and T. J. Lamy, but in all these
volumes the genuine and spurious were juxtaposed with little
serious attempt to separate them out. A useful (and very necessary)
guide to the three Syriac volumes of the Roman edition was provided by F. C. Burkitt in his *S. Ephraim's Quotations from the
Gospels* (Cambridge, 1901), one of the first real efforts to isolate
the genuine works. It was, however, only in the 1950s that reliable
editions of these genuine works, based on the earliest available
manuscripts, started to appear in the *Corpus of Oriental Christian*

Writers (CSCO), published at Louvain in Belgium. The great hymn cycles are now all available in this series, along with several of the verse homilies.

St Ephrem's main works are listed below, with references to translations where available. The following abbreviations are employed:

CSCO = *Corpus Scriptorum Christianorum Orientalium* (the first volume listed contains the text, the second the translation, usually German).

Gwynn = J. Gwynn (ed.), in *Select Library of Nicene and Post-Nicene Fathers,* second series, vol. 13 (1898).

Morris = J. B. Morris, *Select Works of St Ephrem the Syrian* (Oxford, 1847).

PO = *Patrologia Orientalis.*

SS = *Scriptores Syri* (subdivision of CSCO).

The hymn cycles (madrāshē)

1. Hymns on Faith (87 hymns): CSCO 154-5 = SS 73-4. English translation (not always reliable, being based on the poor Roman edition) in Morris. There is a valuable study by E. Beck in *Studia Anselmiana* 21 (1949).
    A more recent translation of nos. 14, 73 and 82 is given in *The Harp of the Spirit;* nos. 10 and 20 are translated by R. Murray in *Eastern Churches Review* 3 (1970) and *Parole de l'Orient* 6/7 (1975/6) respectively, and no. 18 by P. Yousif in *Eastern Churches Review* 10 (1978).

2. Hymns on Nisibis (77 hymns): CSCO 218-9, 240-1 = SS 92-3. English translation of nos. 1-21, 35-42 and 52-68 in Gwynn, and of 36, 50, 52 and 69 in *The Harp of the Spirit.*

3. Hymns against Heresies (56 hymns): CSCO 169-70 = SS 76-7.

4. Hymns on Virginity (52 hymns): CSCO 223-4 = SS 94-5. English translation of no. 31 by R. Murray in *Sobornost/ Eastern Churches Review* 1 (1979); of 7 and 33 in *The Harp of the Spirit.*

5. Hymns on the Church (52 hymns): CSCO 198-9 = SS 84-5. English translation of no. 9 by R. Murray in *Sobornost/ Eastern Churches Review* 2 (1980), and of no. 36 by S. P. Brock in *Eastern Churches Review* 7 (1976).

6. Hymns on the Nativity (28 Hymns): CSCO 186-7 = SS 82-3.

The same volume contains thirteen hymns on Epiphany which are probably not by Ephrem, but nevertheless early. English translations of most of these two collections can be found in Gwynn; no. 11 on the Nativity also appears in *The Harp of the Spirit*.

7. Hymns on Unleavened Bread (21 hymns), on the Crucifixion (9 hymns), and on the Resurrection (5 hymns): CSCO 248-9 = SS 108-9. English translation of the third hymn on Unleavened Bread, and of hymns 1 and 2 on the Resurrection, in *The Harp of the Spirit*.

8. Hymns on Paradise (15 hymns): CSCO 174-5 = SS 78-9. Translated here.

9. Hymns on the Fast (10 hymns): CSCO 246-7 = SS 106-7. English translation of no. 6 in *The Harp of the Spirit*.

10. Hymns preserved only in Armenian (51 hymns): PO 30 (with Latin translation). English translation of no. 49 in *The Harp of the Spirit*.

11. Of doubtful authenticity are the Hymns on Abraham of Qidun and on Julian the Elder (Juliana Saba), in CSCO 322-3 = SS 140-1, and those on the Confessors in CSCO 363-4 = SS 159-60.

Verse homilies (mēmrē)

1. 6 homilies on Faith: CSCO 212-3 = SS 88-9. English translation in Morris. There is an important study by E. Beck in *Studia Anselmiana* 33 (1953).

2. 16 homilies on Nicomedia (preserved only in Armenian): PO 37 (with French translation and extensive introduction).

3. Beck has published a series of volumes containing *mēmrē* attributed to Ephrem, but only a few of these are genuine: Sermones I-IV and *Nachträge zu Ephraem Syrus,* CSCO 305-6 = SS 130-1; CSCO 311-2 = SS 134-5; CSCO 320-1 = SS 138-9; CSCO 334-5 = SS 148-9; and CSCO 363-4 = SS 159-60. Two verse homilies for which there are Greek translations are those on the Sinful Woman and on Jonah, both in *Sermones* II (English translation of the former in Gwynn, and of the latter by H. Burgess, *The Repentance of Nineveh* (London, 1853); the Greek text of the homily on Jonah is published in *Le Muséon* 80 (1967), reproduced in *Iōnas Ephraim tou Surou*

(Athens, 1984)). A translation of one of the homilies on the Virgin in *Nachträge* is provided in *The Harp of the Spirit*.

Works in artistic prose

1. Homily on our Lord: CSCO 270-1 = SS 116-7. English translation in Gwynn.
2. Letter to Publius: in *Le Muséon* 89 (1976), with English translation.

Prose works

1. Commentary on Genesis and Exodus: CSCO 152-3 = SS 71-2. An unpublished English translation of Comm. on Genesis by Katharine Refson is on deposit in the Bodleian Library, Oxford (MLitt. thesis, 1982); Spanish translation by A. Peral Torres (Madrid, 1978). Section II (on Gen. 2-3) is translated here.
2. Commentary on the Diatessaron: CSCO 137, 145 = Scr. Armeni 1-2 (complete text in Armenian translation), and L. Leloir, *Saint Ephrem, Commentaire de l'Évangile concordant* (Dublin, 1963), with an edition of what remains of the Syriac original. Complete French translation in *Sources chrétiennes* 121.
3. Commentaries on Acts and the Pauline Epistles (preserved only in Armenian). Only Latin translations are available, of the former in F. J. Foakes Jackson and K. Lake, *The Beginnings of Christianity,* vol. 3 (London, 1926), and of the latter by the Mekhitarist Fathers (Venice, 1893).
4. Other commentaries, on Old Testament books, are attributed to Ephrem, but most of these are not by him.
5. Polemical works: C. W. Mitchell, *S. Ephraim's Prose Refutations,* 2 volumes (London, 1912, 1921), with English translations.

Among the inauthentic prose works attributed to Ephrem is an interesting letter to mountain ascetics (CSCO 334-5 = SS 148-9).

[An extensive selection of hymns in English translation ca now be found in K. E. McVey, *Ephrem the Syrian: Hymns* (Classics of Western Spirituality, 1989)].

Index 1: Biblical References

(To the Hymns   Hymn and Stanza, R = Response)

234

Index 2: Proper Names

Index 3: Subjects

Abyss I.12.13
Adam as image VI.5, XII.15, XIII.4; as king III.14, XIII.3.4.6.
Altar I.9
Angel (Watcher) VI.20.23.24, VII.8.15; C.18
Animals II.12, III.4, VI.20, XII.16.19.20, XIII.3.5.7.10; C.4.9-11.
    13.15.18.29.33
Apostle I.7.14, VI.22, VII.15, XI.14; C.27
Ark I.10, II.12.13, XIV.5
Ark of Covenant VI.1
Birds II.12, III.4; C.9.10
Bitter, bitterness VI.9, VII.6.14, IX.2, X.15, XI.10, XII.3, XV.12.
    13.15
Body III.6.12.14, V.8, VI.23, VII.1.5.12.19, VIII.2-9.11, IX.13.16.
    18-21.23; C.14
Boundary (barrier, enclosure, fence; *syaga*) I.13, II.7, III.3,
    IV.1.6-8, V.15, VII.26-8, VIII.11, XI.3.13; C.7.
Breeze, wind III.2, IX.7-13, XI.12
Bridal chamber (*gnona*) I.6, VII.15.24, XIII.3.10.
Bridge V.4.5.
Captive, captivity, servitude I.13, V.13.14, VII.31, XIII.4.9.10,
    XIV.1-3.6.15, XV.9
Chariot I.7, VI.23
Children I.13, IV.10, V.14, VII.7-9, VIII.5, IX.1, X.12.13,
    XIV.10.13; C.30.32.
Church II.13, VI.7.9.10, XI.2
Cloud I.5.7, II.9, VI.23, IX.5, X.15, XV.5.15
Colors IV.7, V.6, VI.2, IX.27, X.10, XI.7, XV.1
Commandment III.3.5.9.13; C.7-9.14.17-21.23.26.31.32.35
Contest, struggle III9, VI.18.24, VII.2.23, IX.1, XII.17; C.16-18.22
Cross VI.R.5, IX.2, XII.10
Crown I.9, II.7, III.9, V.5.6, VI.1.12.24, VII.3.15.19.23.24.28,
    IX.1.2, X.3.7, XII.17.18, XIV.8.13
Curse VI.8, VII.8.14, IX.1.12, XI.9.11.13, XII.3.14, XIII.5,
    XIV.4.15; C.6.23.29-31.35